IF WE ARE TO BECOME

A conversation taking us to the next level

Ruramai Sithole

DEFINITION

Become

/bɪˈkʌm/

Definition: begin to be.

Verb:..become;

3rd person present:....................becomes;

Past tense:...became;

Gerund or present participle...............becoming;

Past participle.....................................become.

This page was intentionally left blank.

For all the dreamers out there – me included.

This page was intentionally left blank.

CONTENTS

Detailed Contents

PROLOGUE

The Becoming of this book

My story

June 2019...

Until now, I hadn't quite understood the phrase "Identity Crisis." It was only after I experienced it that I got a handle on it. If you, yourself, don't know what "Identity Crisis" is, then I'll give you the definition from the Oxford English Dictionary. *"It is a period of uncertainty and confusion in which a person's sense of identity becomes insecure, typically due to a change in their expected aims or role in society."*

The key terms here are **uncertainty, confusion, insecurity, expected aims**, and **role in society.**

During this period of my life, I had just finished college, and I was awaiting graduation. One would expect me to be elated and enthralled to be graduating, but unfortunately, that wasn't the case for me.

For starters, I found myself in a place of isolation that I was unaccustomed to. We finished our final semester in May 2019, but I needed to remain on campus long after the majority of the students had left. This was because I was part of the Students' Representative Council. I, with three other executive members of the council, had to stay behind until we had handed over our responsibilities to the incoming student leaders.

To be entirely honest with you, when I was asked to stay behind, I happily accepted this duty because it meant I wouldn't be home. Not that I hated home, but the amount of laborious work I had to do on my dad's farm is what I hated.

The elections for the new council were to be held in October, and there were a good five months ahead of me – which seemed short at the time. But as soon as every other student left, the days became longer than usual. This was the first time in my four years as a college student that I actually felt alone. If you have never been alone, let me tell you this; a lot of things happen when you are in solicitude. By things, I mean 'thinking'.

Drowned in my thoughts –it suddenly dawned upon me that where I was going was obscured with **uncertainty**. It hit me in the face (baammmm!!), and just like that, I realized how unsure I was of what lay ahead of me. Compounded by the fact that I was in one of the world's poorest countries (Zimbabwe[1]), I had not the slightest idea of how the future was going to play out for me. Sure, I was going to have a degree in 5-months' time, but would it mean anything in a country with such a staggering high unemployment rate? Would I be able to lead a comfortable life, marry, support my family, and, most of all, would I be happy? All these questions roamed about in my head.

After questioning my future and seeing how uncertain it was, I went on to interrogate my past (another bad idea). As I questioned myself further, not only did I fail to find the answers, but I also became **confused**. I was confused about whether or not what I did in the past was worth it. What if it was all for nothing? What if I had done this and that instead? Would I have had a much more unobstructed view of my future?

From this ordeal, I learned that when you look into the future and stay there for too long, you become anxious. And, on the other hand, if you dwell in the past, you'll often more be regretful (at least in my personal experience).

This was me on my self-imposed isolation, oscillating between uncertainty and confusion – back 'n forth. And, because this oscillation was not put to a halt, it spiraled into insecurity.

Once I lost sense of my future and my past, I became insecure. I wasn't confident of where I had come from and where I was going.

This insecurity birthed two problems;

1) I became aimless, and

2) I forgot/lost my role within the societal context.

See, when I became insecure – all that I had previously aimed for became meaningless. The expectations and aims that had driven me no longer made much sense. I no longer needed anything to aim for because let's face it, there was a very high probability that it wasn't going to work out (thoughts of an insecure person). The insecurity drove me to adopt mantras like, "does it matter?", "who cares?" "whatever," etc.

I couldn't find satisfying enough answers to questions about my role in society. What was I born for? Was I on the right path to fulfilling that role? And most of all, given a chance, would I be capable of performing that role? These and other similar questions remained unanswered at that time. At this point, I realized that going home to the farm, wasn't such a bad idea after all.

How & why I wrote the book

But something amazing happened to me in this period. I became more intrigued about myself like never before. It was also at this time that I perhaps asked myself the most important, thought provoking question I had ever asked myself.

What would I need to know, do, or not do for me to step into my next level?

That one question is the seed that birthed this book into existence. Everything in this book revolves around answering that question. I concur with Matt Haig[2] who said, 'every book written is the product of a human mind in a particular state' I had always been big on self-development but when I asked myself that question, I started reading books and listening to talks like I never had before. Not only that, but I started doing all this with so much enthusiasm than I had ever experienced before. I consumed tons of text, audio, and visual self-help material, and one inch at a time, I climbed out of my hells' hole. I learned more about myself and others and it made me significantly more aware.

However, there was something, or rather some advice, I was yearning for that I couldn't find anywhere. I needed someone to tell me what I wanted to hear, but no one seemed to do so. That's how I started waking up early morning to perform rituals like journaling. I would write myself short pieces of advice (solely for my own consumption). I would use these for affirmations, visualizations, or daily mantras. Sometimes it would be random ideas that would surge through my mind. And sometimes it was a synthesized idea from what I had read or heard. I would later research that idea and develop it further to suit and support my own psychological needs.

With time these random unconsolidated and poorly developed ideas turned into a dozen pages that I later looked at and thought to myself, "can't I thoroughly research and consolidate these ideas? Couldn't I develop it into a book?" I wondered.

You might have noticed that I dedicated this book to myself – it is not that I was trying to seem like a total douchebag or something along those lines. I just realized that the Becoming of this book was fueled by the conversations I had with myself when I was having my "identity crisis". So it's a book I wrote so that I could read. The conversations were centered on how I could take myself to the next level. If I Was 'To Become', I wondered, what knowledge would I need to have, what would I need to do, and what would I need to refrain from doing.

Who do I recommend this book to?

I recommend this book to anyone seeking more out of the life they currently have. Someone who has an insatiable need to be his/her "next level person." This someone can be a high school student just wanting to excel in his/her studies. Or a college kid who is trying to navigate his/her way to a desirable and fulfilling destination. It could be the Founder of a startup that is struggling to remain on its feet in this cut-throat world or a CEO of a company/organization that needs to step things up. A retiree trying to recalibrate his/her life might also find this book useful. For a person seeking to thrive in their social domains like relationships and marriages – this book is for you as well. The list of potential wanna-be Becomers is endless. All that matters is you know where you stand and the area of your life that needs to be taken to the next level.

How to use this book

My hope when I wrote this book (and still is) is that the thoughts, ideas, and stories I infused into this book are also being sought by someone else out there. And I hope that person is you.

The truth of the matter is that I am no expert at anything. If you bump into something that sounds deeply meaningful or esoteric, chances are I would have adapted it from someone else's work. And if you find some portions to be immaturely interpreted, then forgive my amateurism.

In any case, you'll still benefit from any outcome because:

1. If you meet something new that challenges your old belief system, then that would be awesome.

2. If you meet what you already know, then your perspective will be confirmed (still a win). And, if;

3. If you find my way of thinking and ideas to be 'wrong' or my interpretations out of context, I will still have succeeded. All I intend to do is to spark a never-ending conversation that can take us to the next level. Even if it has to be a debate. Through

that disagreement, we'll both learn a thing or two from each other.

To get the most out of this book, I would highly suggest that you read it with the perspective that I don't know anything. That I simply want to have a conversation with you, where I lay out stories, thoughts, and ideas for you to think about so you can add your thoughts or subtract some. At the end of our discussion on how we can Become, we will have both a better understanding on the subject matter.

Treat this as one of those conversations with your sibling, mate, work colleague, etc. Casual and impromptu.

You can/should treat this book like a pork rib steak (I love pork ribs, by the way). When served on a Plata, you don't necessarily have to eat everything. Some parts of the steak might be burnt beyond your liking. And some parts of the steak are made of bones. When eating this "pork-rib-steaky-book," you should devour the steak, leave the burnt part, and don't forget to spit out the bones.

CHAPTER ONE

BECOMING

"The only person you are destined to become is the person you decide to be"

\- Ralph Waldo

A man blinded with possibilities

Presenter: It's a chilly spring morning on this runway here and for 33 year old Capetonian, Hein Wagner[1] it's the stuff dreams are made of because today he is attempting to break a land speed record"

Interviewer: Would you say this is the biggest challenge you have undertaken so far?

Hein: Most daring, eeehhhmnn the scariest hhhm and the most hair – raising.

That is an excerpt from the short documentary video[2] from Hein Wagner's attempt to break the world land speed record back on the 8th of September 2005. As Hein himself had put it, it was the most daring, the scariest, and most hair-raising challenge he had decided to lock horns with. All this should already tell you something about Hein. He was a person who had made a hobby of seeking out challenging feats and trying to beat them. It wasn't his first, and you can bet it wasn't going to be his last either.

Succeeding at this attempt would see him being named the first South African to set a world land record. In this case, succeeding meant he had to surpass the current record, which was at that time a staggering high of 223km/h. For such a task, he was going to use a sponsored V8 red Maserati. Hein did the seemingly impossible on a one-kilometer stretch as he clocked a top speed of 269km/h, averaging 242.3 km/h. Hein was now the record holder for the world land speed and the first from South Africa.

I am sure that you are probably not impressed by Hein's top speed because drivers who race in the Formula 1 like Lewis Hamilton[3] reach over 300km/hr. Right? But let me tell you what makes Hein's speed record worth applauding over and over again.

Hein Wagner is blind! (This isn't a typing error)

This record-breaker was born blind and drove that car blind and is still blind to this day. Hein Wagner, a man who was not allowed to drive on any road, is the same guy who broke World Land Speed Record for the blind. As noted earlier, Hein has many records under his belt such as running the Antarctica Marathon, the Two Oceans, and The New York Marathons. He also finished a full Ironman, participated in Cape Town Cycle Tours, and hiked the ten highest mountains in the Western Cape of South Africa. That's not all. He competed in the World Triathlon Series in Cape Town and completed the Cape to Rio Yacht Race, to mention just a few.

From a realistic and perhaps a safety point of view, no one would expect a born-blind person to be seeking out such challenges. But for Hein, it's a different story altogether. As a person who might be viewed as specially-challenged or disadvantaged, he has chosen to live on the edge – a life full of daring, scary, and hair-raising moments.

If put in Hein's shoes, most people would certainly not approach life the same way he does. Many would be mad at life, viewing themselves as victims or with an inferiority complex. They would opt to stay safe indoors and not try anything because being blind would be a good reason to be exempted from living like Hein.

Hein embodies all that it means to Become. This is what Becoming is all about; it is choosing growth and adventure instead of safety and comfort. It is when the world would not expect anything from you, but you go on to achieve the impossible. Becoming is attempting to break world records even if blind and somehow disadvantaged. When society thinks you should be lying on the couch all day at home, petting your guide dog, but you choose to be out there racing at 269km/h, climbing the steepest mountains, and canoeing along rivers. That's what Becoming is.

Is it not sad that many people die in their comfort zones under the pretext that it is safer and more secure than entering into Hein's world? In the world of Becomers, there is a humungous difference between 'merely existing' and 'truly living'.

The Skateboarding Maiden of Finland

For Lena Salmi[4] Becoming means; "riding till she dies" and riding, she does. That is her motto, by the way. Lena is a 67-year old Finnish lady based in Helsinki who dares to take skateboarding as a hobby and a profession. At that age, we might expect her to be in diapers, wearing flip flops and basking all day at some old people's home. The common perception would be that she is frail, slow at thinking, and amnesiac. But that is not for Lena.

Lena happens to be one of the highest-profile skateboarders in the world and has taught many more people to become skateboarding professionals. What is incredible is that not only is she, in society's' view, "too old" for such an extreme activity, but that she only started skating at the age of sixty-one.

Her courage is something worth talking about because let's face it; you don't find so many pips at that age getting involved in such teenage-like activities. I mean, even as young as I am, I am terrified of skating. (Side story: the one time I tried it, it didn't go so well).

It requires another level of courage to be able to take the bull by its horns in a similar fashion to Lena. Despite her age and even gender, Lena bulldozed her way to becoming a top skating professional in Finland and perhaps in the world. She did all this, withstanding critics, cynics, and scornful people. People who thought her place was in a retirement home rather than in the streets wearing jeans doing some flips with a skateboard. But here she was, still growing older and still skating.

In her own words, *"If I think that I am getting afraid of getting old, then I can't live"*. She, clearly, is not allowing her age or any form of fear to stand in her way. She believes that fearing to live can in fact inhibit her from living fully. Lena, the Juggernaut, goes on to say, *"Don't think what other people think. You have to take life into your own hands"*.

When one defines what Becoming means to him/her, and sets out to get it, he/she will sort of morph into an unstoppable being. That person will become a juggernaut that bulldozes everything in its path.

The Skateboarding Maiden of Finland (Lena, 67) is joined in these titan-like ranks by Johanna Quaas[5], a 95-year-old gymnast and Jean Harcourt[6], an 86-year-old marathon runner. And, all these women typify Becoming. They are bold women defying odds, gender and age limit barriers. They are going after what they value and not showing any signs of stopping. In other words, they Became, and they continue Becoming every single day.

The Boy who harnessed the wind

Growing up in Masitala village in Dowa, Malawi, William Kamkwamba[7] grew up in a family overcome with hardships. William's family survived on subsistence crop farming, but in 2001, after being accepted at a secondary school, a famine hit that region. This meant that there wasn't any excess harvest to sell to cover anything other than necessities. In fact, there wasn't enough to feed the family. In this rough time William was forced to drop out of school because his parents could not pay the required eighty dollars (annual) school fees. This was disheartening for someone as keen on learning as William. For a while, he would sneak into the school only to attend the science classes because his dream was to solve the energy crisis that could potentially save his family from the wrath of this famine.

He spent most of his time in the library researching power until he stumbled upon a book called *'Using Energy[8]'*. And upon devouring it, he learned about windmills and that wind energy could be converted to electrical energy.

At the age of only 14 years, William built a wind turbine using material collected from a junkyard. He incorporated a tractor fan blade, old shock absorber, a bicycle, gum tree poles, and an old recycled car battery into his project. William successfully powered light bulbs and managed to charge his neighbors' mobile phones. And that's not all; he managed to upgrade the windmill to pump grey-water for irrigation.

The rest is just history. His fame grew and spread like wildfire. Indeed, the boy had harnessed the wind and triumphed in the face of an impending calamity. Who could have ever thought that a 14-year-old boy would end up harnessing the wind to save an entire community?

When you Become, you start harnessing the unthinkable. You will see opportunities in dark times. When adversity jabs at you, you will not accept it as final. You will soldier on like the soldier you are.

What I found inspiring in William's story is not the erection of the windmill or his perseverance. While that is laudable, of course, there is something priceless that William managed to attain. He got people's attention before he had succeeded. At first, William faced, and had to endure, a lot of skepticism and criticism. At one time, his father tore down his prototype windmill – telling him that it was just a toy, and that he should quit believing in fairytales and dreams. But that did not stop him.

As Ernest Hemmingway[9] noted, *'no one can stop the idea whose time has come'*. The entire village ended up buying into his vision of harnessing the wind. If you watch the movie (The Boy Who Harnessed The Wind), you'll be left awestruck by how much attention William received before even making the actual windmill. That is what happens when you have genuinely Become;

people will readily buy into your vision. Whatever you pursue, those around you will remain entranced and excited to be part of it. You will get support from the most unexpected people of all.

William's father, who had earlier broken down his windmill and called it a toy, was later seen sweating and toiling under the sun, helping his son build it back up (tables do turn around after all). Oh! And remember the bicycle that was part of the windmill? It was not picked up from the scrap yard. It was William's father who donated it towards this windmill construction project.

Are you able to appreciate how big this is? That bicycle was perhaps the most valuable asset William's father owned at that time. Still, he gave it up only for it to be torn apart and be used to build this imaginary power generating solution. Imagine asking your father for his only car so that you can break it and utilize its parts for some crazy project you saw in a secondary school textbook (crazy, right?).

But that is the beauty of Becoming - people will find it easy to buy into your vision. For all those who dream of changing the world or making it a better place – if you focus on Becoming, the rest will fall into place (more on this in Chapter 8).

Unmasking 'Becoming'

All of us share one thing in common, and that is, we are all brought into this world as eggs. Whether we hatch and manifest into something else is entirely up to us. One can choose to stay in the eggshell (the comfort zone) and not go out to face the harsh world. While one can do the exact opposite and break free from that eggshell - going into the unknown in search of his/

her North-Star. One could be physically disadvantaged like Hein, considered too young or too old like Lena. Or one could be facing adversity like William, but still go out to pursue and achieve the unthinkable.

Speaking of eggs, did you know? If you help a chick hatch from the eggshell, that chick will not be as strong as it should be, and its chances of surviving in this harsh world will be slim? And so is Becoming. It's a procedure that needs only you to perform it for yourself. No one can Become for you because it is an inside-out process. What I mean by inside-out is just like how the chick inside the eggshell initiates the hatching process, so must you also initiate Becoming from within. You have to feel the need to Become intrinsically, and then start the process yourself. Once you become on the inside, stepping out of that shell will easy-peasy.

> *If an egg breaks from an outside force*
> *life ends....*
> *If broken by an inside force*
> *Life begins.....*
> *Great things always begin from the inside*
> *– Unknown*

This is in line with the popular adage by Robin Sharma[10] which says, "The door of success does not swing outwards, it only swings inwards". Indeed, 'success' is something we attract – it starts from within. And to be honest, Becoming can be abstractly viewed as being successful in our endeavors. If that is the case, then, it is admissible to rephrase and say, "The door to Becoming does not swing outwards; it only swings inwards".

You Become from the inside.

How do you know if you are Becoming? By merely looking at the direction that the majority of people are headed to, you can easily navigate your way to Becoming. Very few amongst us have the courage it takes to Become. The road to Becoming is one that is least traveled.

In that light, if everyone is headed north, then you need to make a U-turn and start heading south quickly. Those who Become are those who usually choose to go against the grain. They don't follow the multitude. They would rather go through virgin forests and unchartered territories than use the clear and safe roads traveled by everyone.

If you see footprints on the path you are on, the chances are that someone has already been to where you are trying to go. In essence, there won't be anything new to discover there. Let's face it, Vasco Da Gama[11] would not have been the 'Vasco Da Gama' that we know today, had he decided to voyage to a place everyone knew or had already been to. It took exploring parts of the world no one had ever dared to, to be such a well-known explorer.

"Do not go where the path may lead, go instead where this no path and leave a trail."

- Ralph Waldo Emerson.

It is also imperative to note that Becoming is not about reaching a certain point or destination, but it is an unceasing journey. A virtuous cycle and a never-ending road full of ups and downs, unexpected turns, and, most of all, growth. It's not like upon deciding to Become, then all of a sudden you find yourself living in a problem-free world. Unfortunately, that is not the case; it is the direct opposite. If you start seeking more, then expect more problems to start seeking you. That is how it usually plays out.

But for those Becoming, it is through these trials and tribulations that they Become even more. It is in times of adversity that characters are forged. Such is why we have people who never seem to be struck down by anything in life. They are always resilient in times and situations that most of us would throw in the towel.

To be honest, Becoming is a broad subject with many interpretations. Still, for the purpose of this book, we will distill it to *"morphing into the next level"*. Be it as a person, business, organization, or anything else.

Whatever your age or domain of specialization, the goal is always to become better. Not better than anyone, but better than what you were yesterday. Becoming is applicable to different environments, to different age groups, to different agendas, goals, etc. It is relevant to leadership, businesses, family matters, marriages - you name it.

The good news is that the race to Becoming is open to all. Anyone can Become. Anyone, but not everyone! Not everyone has the guts, remember.

No one can define what Becoming means for you. I have given my definition – you are also allowed to interpret it however way you see fit. The bottom line is that it must encapsulate some form of growth and positive movement.

Remember the metaphor we used about eggs earlier? For eggs to hatch, they require some form of heat before the offspring can hatch. This book, I hope, will provide the necessary warmth you need in your life for you to hatch from that eggshell you are in – so you can step onto the next level 'you'. Whether it is in your personal life, business, or any other venture. I hope the ten chapters in this book will take you through an incubation process and assist you towards your hatching.

This book is for individuals who believe they are blind and too disadvantaged. It is for those who have been told that they are too old or young to make a difference. But, they desire to bring forth a positive change, and they want more. This is a guide towards how you can be 'that more,' despite actually being blind, young, old, etc.

Through big ideas, stories, and personal thoughts, I will outlay an argument that can aid you and me towards our Becoming.

I will talk about what we need to know, what we need to do to, and, most importantly, what we don't need to do for us to Become.

Through This Book:
- You will learn why you should Embrace Adversity and how you can do so.
- You will be introduced to The Harsh Reality (all issues pertaining to death, finding your purpose and value in life)
- You will also learn the Laws of Becoming from Isaac Newton.

- You will be taught easy, effective, and proven strategies to beat fear and the existential urge to procrastinate.
- The Truth and What to Trust on your journey towards Next-Level will also be shared in this book.
- You will learn how to Lead as you Become.
- You will better understand Happiness as it is also discussed in this book.
- And so much more.....

Let the games begin........

CHAPTER TWO

THE TRUTH

*"All you need to know and observe in yourself is this:
Whenever you feel superior or inferior to anyone, that's the ego in
you."*

– Eckhart Tolle

You are not Inferior

You learned it...

In the 1970s, an American psychologist named Martin Seligman[1] developed a concept known today as the *'learned helplessness theory[2]'*. He was looking into classical conditioning when he happened to stumble upon this concept. What he learned was that if organisms endured aversive stimuli repeatedly without any way to either control or escape it, the organisms would end up not even to trying to avoid the stimulus.

In simpler layman terms, if an animal or a person underwent something undesirable and painful long enough – that subject would end up becoming accustomed to that pain. It would regard it as final and inescapable. Hence, it would not try to avoid or escape the stimulus it was subjected to and would helplessly take the beating.

He conducted lab tests on various animals – mainly dogs. His experiments involved restraining mongrel dogs and shocking them with electricity. After being electrocuted repeatedly, the dogs would be placed inside cages. The cages were designed in such a way that they had two distinct zones. One side was the electrocution zone while the other was free from electricity. So in essence, to escape and avoid being electrocuted, the dog just had to switch sides.

Instinctually, when the previously electrocuted naive dogs were put into these electrocution zones, they would run around haphazardly trying to avoid the zaps and hoping to even possibly escape. But, this would only last for about 30 seconds, and the dogs would quit running around and lie down and/or start whining as they received the electric shocks. It is like the dogs had given up and made up their minds that this demise was final and there was no escaping from it. Hence, they would give in and be passive as they helplessly took the electric shocks.

On the other hand, when the same experiment was done on a different set of dogs that had not been electrocuted prior to this, they exhibited a different response. They would not accept the electric shocks without putting up a fight. In fact, the dogs would quickly assimilate the fact that if they jumped onto the other side of the cage, they would escape and not receive any shock.

This lab experiment showed that if an organism was put through some traumatic events it had no control over, for long enough, it would affect how it dealt with future traumatic experiences. As shown, its motivation to fight back or avoid it would be diminished.

It's like the dogs, upon realizing how unavoidable the electric shock was, became helpless to the situation. In other words, they had learned to become helpless. Hence the coining of the phrase *"learned helplessness"*.

What we can deduce from this is, for starters, animal rights weren't really a thing back then. Poor creatures, right? Secondly and more importantly, if we take a closer look, we will all agree that how the dogs learned to take in the electric shocks is very much alike to how we have also learned some of our behaviours in the face of negative situations.

When Donald Hiroto[3] carried out this same experiment on college students, the results were similar to those found on dogs and cats. Of course, they weren't electrocuting people, but he made use of a loud aversive noise as the negative experience. Just like the other organisms, people who had been exposed to this loud noise without being provided with a switch to stop it sat passively. They did not try to avoid it even when placed in a different set up where they could have stopped it.

When we go through adversity or face situations that are seemingly insurmountable and unavoidable, we are often left paralyzed and depleted of our fighting spirit. On the surface, it might seem to be the case that we are not in control, and we cannot escape from these situations. But, when the tables turn around, and we gain control, or if the openings to escape are availed, we will most certainly not even notice and take advantage of them. We would have already decided not to try anymore.

In the dog-experiments, the previously electrocuted dogs were submissive in nature when their captors tried to take them out of their cages. They would lie down and not resist. But the non-electrocuted dogs, on the other hand, were aggressive in nature – either barking at or running away from their captors. They acted in direct opposition to their counterparts who had learned to become helpless and submissive in nature.

Learned helplessness can be traced to many human behaviours like poverty, dating, human and drug abuse, politics, discrimination, the way we view achievement, and even depression, only to highlight a few. In the face of uncontrollable situations, if our efforts are futile in providing relief, we eventually give up and take the beating as it comes. This is what they mean when they say, *"what you tell yourself in the face of failure or negative situations determines how well we will cope with the situation."* The narratives we choose to describe these aversive situations play a significant role in how we will behave when faced with similar situations in future. In other words, we can *'learn to be helpless'* if we do not tell ourselves better narratives.

Let us take a look at some real-life instances where learned helplessness is in play:

Politics: Often, people vote because they expect some form of change that will benefit them. But what happens when people have voted countless times and have never received what was promised to them by the politicians? Their motivation towards voting in the future wanes, and the chances of them voting again will be close to zero. Why vote again if nothing is going to change?

Academic achievement: let us say a school kid named John puts in the work and studies hard in an effort to enhance his grades. But, unfortunately, his grades remain in the red zone (maybe because of poor studying skills, lack of resources, etc.). John might end up feeling that he has no direct control over his academic performance. And, if this belief sets in, he will probably not bother study anymore. By doing so, his grades will be affected even more, and this will reinforce the idea that he is not made for school or he is dumb. His motivation will dwindle, and this belief might permeate into other areas of life and end up lowering his self-esteem and self-belief.

Addiction: a person fighting any form of addiction may, after trying to beat it several times, find him/herself back with the addiction. The addicted individual will end up believing he/she is entangled with this addiction for life. You have heard of people who declare themselves powerless to the fangs of addictions. *"I am, and I will always be a smoker"*, they say. *"I just can't help it"*.

Abusive Relationships: have you ever wondered why or how people get caught up in abusive relationships and fail to get out? They may get out, but usually when it's almost too late. Some even go back to their abusers after getting out. This is *'learned helplessness'* in play. A person being abused may come to believe that they cannot escape their abusers even if they really wanted to. Even worse, others come to believe that they deserve the abusive beatings and punishments. You will hear them say, *"He is just short-tempered"*, *"he can't help it"* or *"I really had stepped out of line – I deserved it"*.

This is what you and I have learned. We have learned to become helpless in the face of aversive stimuli. We have learned to synchronize to the pain and negative circumstances. We have learned to acclimate to the situation no matter how aggravating it is. The problem is learning to be helpless in one area seeps into many more areas than we imagine. It is like a drop of ink put into a glass of water. It totally ruins the whole glass of water. This is how the 'inferiority complex' creeps in. As a result, we end up believing that we are inferior in some way.

But, the truth of the matter is;

'You are not inferior!'

This is part of the truth I want you to know. You are not inferior, you were never inferior, and you will never be inferior. If you think you are, then I assure you, you have learned it. And the messed up part about learned helplessness is that it will force you further down.

As Martin Seligman himself suggested, *"In summary, helplessness is a disaster for organisms (people) capable of learning that they are helpless. Three types of disorders are caused by uncontrollability in the laboratory: the motivation to respond is sapped, the ability to perceive success is undermined, and the emotionality is heightened".*

If We Are To Become, then we will all need to understand that there is nothing to be gained nor glory to be found in playing victim, only something to be lost. To Become, we have to eliminate this belief that we are somehow inferior. We will have to avoid entertaining self–limiting thoughts that draw us towards becoming helpless. Lying down, complaining and passively taking beatings of any kind will not get us there. Never has and never will.

Stay motivated to act no matter what, make sure you view success of any sort, as attainable and be emotionally tough.

Believe in your abilities and escape life's electrocutions.

But remember also...

You are not Superior

The boy who flew too close to the sun

Legend has it that:

On the island of Crete, which was surrounded by the Aegean Sea, lived an engineer named Daedalus. Daedalus was a well-famed inventor during his time and a father to Icarus. Daedalus loved his son dearly, and the two were inseparable.

King Minos, the ruler of Crete at that time, gave Daedalus a task to build a maze-like prison, from which not even one person nor monster could escape from. With the assistance of King Minos' slaves, Daedalus built the infamous labyrinth – an intricate maze of tunnels and passages that looked similar and confusing. It is claimed that this labyrinth was so humungous and complex to the extent that even if a hundred men were to be put into this stronghold and wandered off on separate routes not even one of them could ever meet the other again.

Daedalus enjoyed the rewards bestowed upon him for successfully completing this task, and his fame continued to grow like wildfire. He lived in full service to King Minos and was highly favoured. However, Daedalus, through his inventions and popularity, became full of pride and compared himself to the gods. Such pride did not go unnoticed by King Minos, who was maddened and infuriated over Daedalus' behaviour. And, it was decided that it was time for Daedalus to taste his own medicine.

So he cast the man and his son into the labyrinth.

Daedalus took with him a ball of thread, and he tied one end at the labyrinth's entrance, and he used it to find his way out of this maze (after a long struggle of course). But even after finding a way out of the labyrinth, an obstacle lay in their way. Without a boat, how would they get off the island surrounded by the sea?

Daedalus, being an inventor and a thinker, decided he would make wings from bird feathers, wax and thread. He successfully made two pairs of wings that could sustain human flight.

Before they took off Daedalus advised his son; "But mind, Icarus, my son, don't fly too low, too near to the sea, for the feathers once wet will not carry you. But then do not fly too high, too near to the sun, for the sun's heat will, like the lamp's, melt the wax, and make the feathers fall away."

Icarus wasn't listening, he was impatiently waiting to sail across the sky (I cannot blame him though– imagine being the first mortal man to fly). Everything went according to plan, but however, at the peak of their flight Icarus became over exultant, and he flew higher and higher. Full of himself and the wings' capabilities he soared on higher and higher, forgetting his fathers' advise not to fly too high.

Eventually, the wax that had kept the feathers intact melted and Icarus fell into the sea and died.

– Daedalus and Icarus[4]

Imagine after escaping a once deemed inescapable prison and doing it in so much style as flying across the sea. Not in a plane but by wings made out of bird feathers, wax and thread, only to die because you failed to follow a simple instruction! There are innumerable morals to enact from Icarus' story but what stood out for me was how sometimes we doom ourselves into failing because we've overstated our abilities, strengths etc.

Icarus, after tasting freedom, became over ecstatic and overconfident. He forgot or perhaps chose to disregard his father's warning on flying too high – too close to the sun.

If you think about it – this is not really different from how we conduct our daily lives. We tend to forget the ceiling levels to what we can do in life. When we look at ourselves, we would want to think of ourselves as invincible superheroes that are unstoppable. On the surface, this seems healthy or rather the proper mindset to attack life with. Some coin it as being optimistic or highly-motivated.

While there is nothing wrong with being optimistic, the dangers only start to be seen when we lose a total sense of proportion. This happens once we start feeling like we are the Captain America[5] of life and our optimism starts clouding our judgment. When our self-opinion gets in the way of what's practically attainable and what's not. It's one thing to be optimistic and another to be pragmatically optimistic. Being pragmatically optimistic is when you manage to detach yourself from situations and assess them from a realistic point of view without letting emotions cloud you.

This is why Robert Greene included this as a rule in his book *'The Laws of Human Nature'*, when he said, *"Know your limits[6]"*. But knowing our limits is not easy, Robert! We are naturally inclined to keep flying higher and higher like Icarus until the wax binding our wings melts and we fall out of the sky. This sort of challenges the conventional advice we often receive. Many at times we are told that *"we can do anything, we are unstoppable, unbeatable"* etc.

Having an inflated sense of self has and still continues to bring people back to earth in a very humbling way. It is imperative that one keeps him/herself in check against grandiosity. Because, even Jocko and Leif[7] succinctly argued that; *"Ego clouds and disrupts everything: the planning process, the ability to take good advice, and the ability to accept constructive criticism. It can stifle someone's sense of self-preservation. Often the most difficult ego to deal with is your own"*

With that said, *If We Are To Become*, then we will have to get rid of the ideology that we are superior to others in any way. We must never at any time entertain such a thought as it will result in a much more spectacular downfall than Icarus'. Wanting more and believing in ourselves is the key message in this book, but if at any time I sound like I am psyching you up beyond what is realistic, then pardon me.

And as magnificently put forward by Robert Green: *'We humans have a deep need to think highly of ourselves. If that opinion of our goodness, greatness, and brilliance diverges enough from reality, we become grandiose. We imagine our superiority. Often, a small measure of success will elevate our natural grandiosity to even more dangerous levels. Our high self-opinion has now been confirmed by events. We forget the role that luck may have played in the success, or the contributions of others. We imagine we have the golden touch. Losing contact with reality, we make irrational decisions. That is why our success often does not last. Look for the signs of elevated grandiosity in yourself and in others—overbearing certainty in the positive outcome of your plans; excessive touchiness if criticized; a disdain for any form of authority. Counteract the pull of grandiosity by maintaining a realistic assessment of yourself and your limits. Tie any feelings of greatness to your work, your achievements, and your contributions to society'.*

Remember:

You are not superior.
You never were.
You never will be.

But if you think you are, then my advice is that you make sure the wax and thread on your wings is stronger than that which was on Icarus', because you are really flying high – too close to the sun.

Then what are you?

If you remember Daedalus' words to Icarus before they flew across the sky, he said, *"But mind, mind, Icarus, my son, don't fly too low, too near to the sea, for the feathers once wet will not carry you. But then do not fly too high, too near to the sun, for the sun's heat will, like the lamps, melt the wax, making the feathers fall away."*

You see, already Daedalus told us what to do. We should not fly too low and not too high, either. If you fly too low, you'll get wet, and if you fly too high, the wax will melt.

The first half of the truth is that you and I, and everyone else you know is not inferior in any way. In that same light, no one is superior either. Playing victim, blaming others, coming up with excuses, and always whining about how bad things are or how disadvantaged you are, is not really a thing. Just like how thinking highly of yourself, overstating your capabilities, regarding yourself as some god-like mythical figure is equally not a thing.

It would be best if you remain attuned to this fact; that you are not inferior and you are not superior either. You are somewhere in between these two extreme ends. Well, at least, that is where you should be. *"Whenever you feel superior or inferior to anyone, that's the ego in you"*, says Eckhart Tolle[8].

Mark Manson[9] said it less politely. He said, *"You are not special"* and I can't help but concur with him. Just because you regard yourself as an inferior or superior does not make you deserving of any special treatment. Having a sense of entitlement means that you believe you should be treated differently from other people.

And when you are entitled, Mark goes on to highlight that you will either think that:

1. You are awesome, and everyone else sucks, so you deserve special treatment. Or,

2. You suck, and everyone else is awesome, so you deserve special treatment.

Those who are entitled operate in either one of these two mindsets or even oscillate periodically between the two.

There are gradations of course, to how one feels to be either inferior or superior but the truer self is one that exists when the two are balanced. You can think of yourself as a car travelling through a bustling and chaotic road. If you go too slow, you will delay traffic and risk being insulted by other drivers who are in a hurry. You will be hooted at or even bumped into. Going too fast doesn't cut it either, because you will risk yourself getting speed tickets or getting involved in accidents. If Daedalus had escaped with a car, he would have advised his son, *"not too slow, not too fast"*.

The car's speedometer can be a representation of our "reality self-check". We can use it to determine the level of inferiority or superiority we should entertain.

Your imaginary reality self-check should look like the one below:

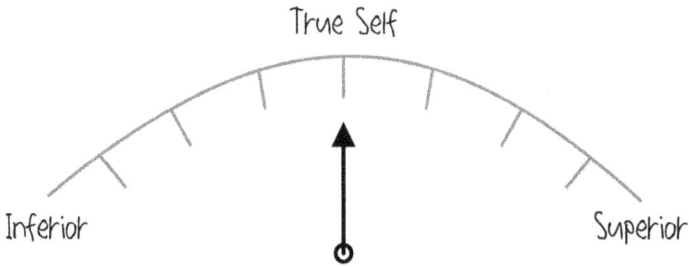

Advice: Keep your pointer as far away from both extreme ends.

Chapter Summary

The Truth

You are not inferior.

You are not worse than anyone.

You are not superior.

You are not better than anyone.

What you should do:

Mantain a healthy balance between Superiority and Inferiority.

CHAPTER THREE

NEWTON'S LAWS OF BECOMING

"Truth is ever to be found in simplicity, and not in the multiplicity and confusion of things."

– Isaac Newton

Before we go anywhere, allow me to make this proposition: I think physics is one of the most challenging fields of study. Having said that, I feel much relieved to point out that physics gave me a tough time back in high school, and if I am not mistaken, I got my lowest grades in Physics. I don't know why Isaac Newton[1] would say, *"Truth is ever to be found in simplicity, and not in the multiplicity and confusion of things"* when all I felt during physics lectures was confusion. However, don't let this give you an attitude towards my desire to teach you a little bit of Physics.

Isaac Newton is credited with coming up with many inventions and scientific theorems that I can't even pretend to understand at this very age. For some reason, out of everything I learned about physics and Newton, I still remember his *'3 Laws of Motion[2]'*. These Laws revolutionized the perception people had with regard to moving objects.

When you think about it, we're also moving objects. Well, at least we should be. For us to step into our next level, we are going to have to be in motion. We will have to move from one point to another. It is prudent then, that we understand these Laws of Motion and be aided by them as we move towards our next level.

1st Law of Becoming

One day I found myself in a heated argument with a friend. I cannot remember how it started, but all I know is she was saying something like, *"We should not worry about anything. Everything will always work out".* What my friend was saying is in line with the popular adage that says, *'good things come to those who wait.'*

That! Right there, dear reader is indisputably the biggest, fattest lie ever told. Good things never come to those who wait. Good stuff only comes to those who act. In fact, good things never come to anyone. Good things elude people, and they ought to be hunted down. History is filled with innumerable men and women of great achievements. These great historical figures are revered to the point of almost being worshipped. And, what enabled these greats to stand out is their ability to spot a problem and after realizing such – they went on to fix it.

They are not remembered because they hoped that somehow the problems would miraculously disappear. No! They did something about it, and they did not wait. That something they did is what shaped the world and has stood the test of time is unforgettable. Had they believed that, somehow, by hoping things were going to change for the better miraculously, the world would not be what it is today.

This then brings us to Mr Isaac Newton. Newton suggested that every body would remain in its state of motion unless an external force acted on it. Meaning, a rolling ball could roll on forever if all external forces were removed. The only reason why a rolling ball will either roll faster, slow down, or even stop is because an external force has come into play.

However, since I am no Physicist, I will rephrase that Law to suit what we are trying to solve through this book (How To Become).

Everything will remain as it is unless something is done about it. Simple logic has it, that nothing will change in your life unless something is done to force a change. Your financial state of affairs, your marriage, your business, your health, all of it, will remain as it is until something is done about it. It is no rocket science that what is happening today in your life, is what will be happening tomorrow unless something different is done today to break the cycle.

This explains why people keep carrying forward their new years' resolutions to the following year. It is not because the resolutions are out of this world or unattainable – it is usually only a matter of doing things the same way and expecting different results.

However, allow me to make a further alteration on this Law:

> *1st Law of Becoming: everything will remain as it is unless YOU DO something about it.*

See, so much of what is happening in your life is based on what you are doing. Only you have the capacity to change what needs to be changed in your life. If you are broke today, you'll remain broke until you do something about it. If you don't do something to either fix or change it, it will remain as it is. If your body does not please you, it will remain in that state unless you go on a diet or you hit the gym. You'll remain an addict until you work on breaking that addiction. It is that simple and irrefutable.

This is what they mean when they say; *'the best way to predict the future is by creating it'*. We should know by now that what we did yesterday led to what we have today and what we are doing today will determine what we will have tomorrow. In that same regard, if what we currently have is undesirable – then according to the 1st Law of Becoming it will remain as awful as it is until we do something to change it.

Back in High School, I always looked forward to the morning assemblies. Well, not all of them but those which the schools' Principal chaired. He always had these long stories to narrate which he thought us students would extract morals from. I don't remember ever paying attention to his stories. However, my beloved wise Principal had a signature-statement that he always dropped off at the end of every story. Back then, that statement never made much sense.

He would conclude by saying; *"Like I always tell to you boys and girls, the destiny lies in your own hands"*.

I never really managed to grasp the gravity of that statement until years later after graduating from his school. To me, he was monotonous and seemed to be trying to sound like someone full of wisdom.

What I didn't realize was that my Principal was telling us what I would later preach about in my first book, just packaged differently. He was, in simplicity, saying whether good things happen to us or not; it is all dependent on us.

If anything amazing is ever going to happen in your life, it is all on you. Truth of the matter is, good, awesome, amazing things ... whatever you prefer calling them, do exist. But the mundane truth is, whether these desirable things are attained or not, lies in your own hands. Now let me ask you, are you going to act or are you going to wait?

The destiny lies in your own hands.

You are either going through life waiting, wishing, hoping you had this and that. Or, you are going after the awesomeness that is waiting for you to tap into. I hope you choose the latter instead of the former.

I pray you are not going to be like those dwelling under the misconception that good things come to them if they wait. If you are waiting for good things to come your way. If you are waiting for your boss to summon you to his office - to hand you over that promotion or pay-raise. If you are waiting to lose that gargantuan tummy that you hate so much. If you are like some, who are waiting for love to walk straight into their lives. If you are just waiting and hoping, then I hate to be the mouthpiece to bad news; it is never going to happen – it's a lie. Nothing will happen unless you make it happen!

2nd Law of Becoming

If you recall, the *1st Law of Becoming* highlighted the need to do something for there to be a change of state in our lives. Any form of change that you yearn for requires you to do something. Otherwise nothing will change.

Before I propose the second law, perhaps let us first define a few key terms.

The change that occurs after we have done something can be thought of as an acceleration (**a**). Let us put it this way; the results of our actions is what we are referring to as acceleration. The acceleration is not the actual action, but the result of an action. For example, practicing yoga and meditating is an action that results in a personal health acceleration. Increasing your monthly income is a financial acceleration. Having more time to dedicate to your family and loved ones is another form of acceleration. Feeling healthier, more refreshed and less stressed can be perceived as other forms of acceleration.

That something which you need to do in order to effect change is the Force applied (**f**). Force is the actual action taken or which needs to be taken to change something. Waking up daily to hit the gym is a form of a force (f). So is cutting off the people that drag you astray from your goals. Studying is a force. Putting yourself on a strict diet is also another form of a force.

The size/value/weight of the objective or goal being sought after is the mass (m). In so saying, m varies depending on what needs to be changed. Losing one kilogram will obviously take less effort than losing ten kilograms. This then means the (**m**) denoting losing one kilogram is less than the (m) for ten kilograms. The (m) resembling running ten kilometres daily is more than the (m) for running just one kilometre.

Back to Isaac Newton again; he went on to allude that the acceleration of a body was directly proportional to the force applied and inversely proportional to the mass of the body(**a=F/m**).

In laymans terms; the bigger the force acting on a body, the bigger the acceleration and conversely, the bigger the mass of the object, the smaller the resultant acceleration.

In that same spirit, the 2nd Law of Becoming will be:

> *The change of state that occurs in our lives is directly proportional to the force we apply and inversely proportional to the size/value/weight of the goal being pursued.*

For any required form of change (acceleration), it will be dependent on the force exerted and the size of the desired change or goal.

The first part of the law is: (**a=f**)..

That is, the bigger and the bolder the action, the bigger the resultant change. All things being constant, the more you study, the more you will improve your grades. The harder and more constantly you exercise, the more you will be fitter, healthier and perhaps even sexier. In a way, this takes us back to the 1st Law of Becoming, because when Force (f) becomes zero, meaning when you do nothing, then, the acceleration (a) also becomes zero.

Because acceleration (a) is always equal to the force (f) applied. Where there is no force, there will be no acceleration (1st Law).

There is a scripture in the Bible that supports this part of the law which says:

You reap what you sow.

–Galatians[3]

In other words if you don't sow, then you can't expect to reap.

The second part of the law is: acceleration of a body is inversely proportional to its mass($a=1/m$). Broken down to the basics, the bigger the mass the smaller the acceleration.

Aligning it to us; the bigger the goal, the challenge or objective, then the less likely it will be easily attainable. A notable change is likely to be attained on a simple challenge, or a small goal. In simplicity, it takes less to meet small objectives, to realize small goals or overcome trivial challenges. It is easier to increase your yearly income by ten percent than it is to increase it by a hundred percent. The ten percent change of state is more easily attainable than the hundred percent change of financial state.

The one time I tried it out, going to the gym didn't go so well. My plan was to gain some muscle and abs in the shortest time possible. I hoped to enter the gym looking as skinny as I am and come out looking like John Cena[4] within a week and then probably look like Dwayne The Rock Johnson[5] by the following month. You can imagine how disappointed I was after a month of painstaking exercise when I came out still looking like me. The only change was that my body and muscles ached so badly. The goal I had set out to achieve and the time allocated were incongruous, and for that reason, my gym experience was the worst. I could have enjoyed the gym and benefited more had I understood the *2nd Law of Becoming*. If only I had understood that because the goal was big (to be like The Rock), it was going to take more than just a month.

If We Are To Become, we have to quit seeking instant gratification and desire the benefits of long term commitment. Wanting it now or acquiring immediate results is not for Becomers. All those who have genuinely Become understand that real change takes more resources, more dedication and more time.

To flog a dead horse one more time; the two variables that determine how much change occurs in our lives are:

1. The force applied (how much we apply ourselves to it).

2. Size of desired goal (how big the task at hand is).

3rd Law of Becoming

Thirdly, Newton added that action and reaction were always equal and opposite.

The 3rd Law of Becoming has a two-fold interpretation.

1st Interpretation – Opposition.

Everyone who understands or who has ever played the game of sport, particularly the one with people teamed up against each other, and there is contact between them, knows this for a fact. The key player is always the most guarded and most fouled person on the pitch.

If you watch soccer, you'd know that Lionel Messi[6] or Christiano Ronaldo[7] are always the targeted men on the pitch. They will usually have two or even more defenders assigned to them to thwart their efforts. In basketball, the likes of Stephen Curry[8], Lebron James[9], and James Harden[10] etc. are always heavily guarded and kept off the ball at all costs. The opponents understand that if the ball gets to these star players, they can easily score goals.

Check this also with rugby, netball, football, hockey, handball etc. I am pretty much convinced that you'll discover this same pattern as well. As a game plan or tactic it kind of makes so much sense to stop the opponent's most influential player. Cripple their star, or their key player, then you stand a chance against the opponent. After all, Robert Greene[11] highlighted this in his book as Law 32 of Power: *Strike the shepherd and the sheep will scatter.* By investing effort to stopping that deadly player, you are in essence striking their shepherd and in effect forcing them (the sheep), to scatter.

I want you to think of life as a game of sport. You, of course, come in as the star player of your life and the main character. Your teammates, the people who wish you well, who want the best out of you, are normally your friends, family and loved ones. And lastly, it can never be a game without an opponent, and this is where all those that wish you to fail, your competitors etc. come into play.

The more threatening you seem towards your opponents, the more they will strive to foul and stop you, or even team up against you. The more you look like a Christiano or a Lebron in this game of life, the more they will heavily guard you against scoring. The more you force to get in, the more they will try to force and keep you out.

This essentially defines the first half of Newton's 3rd Law of Motion:

Action and reaction are always opposite.

If you are progressing forward, expect an equally opposing force to push backwards. You see, the more you set out to achieve great things, the more everything and everyone will seem to be against you. But understand this, my dear friend; each time you find yourself facing opposition, let it serve as an indicator that you are actually doing something right. Because where there is an action, there will be an opposing reaction.

Newton had it that, for example, the faster the ball was travelling through the air, the more backward forces (air resistance) will be acting on that same ball. The more force you apply to push an object lying on the ground, the more the frictional force will act in the opposite direction.

You know what they always say; *'If you have no haters, then you have to up your game'.*

Many of us when faced with opposing reactions, we seem to shrink under this seemingly insurmountable force. We give in to the pressure, when in fact we should be happy and invigorated because it shows that we are doing something. We need a better interpretation of these inevitable situations. If you weren't moving forward, then you would not be facing the opposition you are facing right now.

Let every opposing reaction you face serve as an indicator that someone has noticed your actions. And also whenever you act, expect to face an opposing response.

2nd Interpretation – Equal consequences

Let me tell something you already know; if you touch a hot stove, you will get burnt. If you drink contaminated water, you obviously get sick. If you play in the cold, you'll catch a cold. If you get enough sleep, you'll stay sharp and less stressed. You practice success habits; you attain success in your life. You study, you pass. And so on.

Remember, for every action; there is an **equal** and opposite reaction. In this case, the reaction is a consequence. With that said, the second interpretation of the third law is:

Actions reap relatively equal consequences.

This interpretation should act as a guideline as to how we do what we do. It should also serve as a reminder that whatever we do has equal consequences. Just like how touching a stove will result in a burning consequence and how eating healthy foods will make you healthier.

As we journey along this road to Become, I want this law to guide our actions to be those that produce desirable consequences. Knowing this inalienable truth, that actions give birth to consequences, is agreeing to Steve Covey[12] when he said, *"we need to begin with the end in mind".* In other words, before acting, one needs to look at the possible outcomes or consequences attached to that action. Before touching the hot plate on the stove, think of the consequences and believe me you, if you do so, you might save yourself from an awful burn.

What is commonly known as the *"Karma[13] Effect"* is a version of this action vs. reaction law. The belief that how you treat others will eventually find its way back to you. It is commonly said: *be kind to people you meet on your way up the ladder because you will meet them on your way down.* More like, how you act towards people will determine how they will react back to you.

Using other people as stepping stones towards the attainment of your success has its own equally matching consequences attached to it. The time delay between action and consequence is neither uniform nor predictable. But, what is certain, is that consequences will result no matter how long the time delay. The art of Becoming has this law at heart. If you disregard other people on your way towards Becoming, if your actions are hurtful and demeaning towards others, then in actuality, you are not Becoming.

Yes, you might be climbing a ladder, but that ladder you're climbing will be leaning on the wrong wall. I am urging you to act in such a way that the resultant consequences will be desirable. I want you to pay attention to your actions so that you reap the intentional and beneficial results.

Another way you can look at this action vs. consequence ideology is in light of reverse engineering[14]. No one can dismiss the fact that reverse engineering has aided humankind to advance in technology, health, agriculture etc. However, if you look closely at its core, this concept observes the law of action and consequences. In essence, reverse engineering is knowing the consequence (result) and working to achieve it in reverse. Think of it as working your way backwards. Instead of acting first and waiting for results, you start by thinking of the results, and acting accordingly. That's reverse engineering for you!

The Law of Cause and Effect[15] states that; *'for every effect, there is a definite cause'*. Likewise, for every cause, there is a definite effect. This is just another way of saying your actions have absolute consequences.

In summation, the 2nd Law of Becoming has it that:

Actions have equal and opposing reactions, and the Law can be split into two sub laws:

1. If you are progressing forward, then expect an equally opposing force.
2. Actions reap relatively equal consequences.

Chapter Summary

Laws of Becoming

1st Law of Becoming

Everything will remain as it is unless you do something about it.

2nd Law of Becoming

Any form of change (acceleration) it will be dependent upon the force exerted and the size of the desired change or goal.

3rd Law of Becoming

Action and reaction are always equal and opposite

CHAPTER FOUR

TO AVOID NOT DOING

"The most effective way to do it, is to do it."
                                        – Amelia Earhart

In the previous chapter, we talked about waiting, and I hope we all concurred that waiting would never get us to where we dream of going. Only action will get us there.

Let us say you always make decisions to go after your dreams, but you still end up hesitating. You always get caught up in never-ending cycles of almost acting and back to waiting, over and over again. You often get inspired and motivated to chase down your goals after listening to a talk or reading a book. And still, before acting, you lose that motivation again.

What usually happens after figuring out and deciding what we want to pursue is, we realize the existence of a 'potential gap.' The 'potential gap' is the distance between where we are and where we dream of being. Scrutinizing this gap can be demoralizing, and usually, this is where the battle is lost before it even begins. In our minds, we become convinced that we are trying to build castles in the air.

How then do we overcome the 'potential gap'? One way to do so is through motivation. With the right amount of motivation, we can pursue anything no matter how distant it might be. But that's the problem; we can't rely on something that can falter anytime. We cannot guarantee that we are going to be motivated every step of the way. What happens when our motivation well runs dry?

What's worse is that motivation only works when the going is easy. Once the doo-doo hits the fan, it takes something more than just mere motivation to remain persistent. Motivation surely works, but only to a certain extent.

A different form of motivation, called drive, is needed. Drive transcends any and every obstacle you might think of. Do not let the phrase 'drive' scare you away. When defined loosely, drive is just motivation with sound techniques to keep you at it even when you no longer feel like doing it or you don't see a way out.

This chapter was put in place to equip you with a few techniques to help you take the road to Becoming dauntlessly and without looking back. In essence, today, we are going to learn to create our own drive. We are going to instill ourselves with the confidence to squarely face our 'potential gaps' and not back off.

The beauty of the human mind, which again poses as a problem, is that it believes every narrative it is told. Our minds can entertain stories, and if these stories are repeated often enough, we end up believing them. This means that, the mind, if told lies enough times, it will adopt them as the truth, and if told the truth without conviction, it may fail to believe it.

Put yourself in a Skinner Box.

Has it ever occurred to you that our acquired tastes and preferences, habits, behaviours, aversions, etc. are all acquired through some form of learning? One of the ways we learn is through conditioning, either classical[1] or operant[2] conditioning.

I want to propose that we use operant conditioning to learn how to fight self-limiting beliefs that continuously hold us back when we try to progress forward. Operant conditioning is based on a bit of manipulation. It's a learning process whereby responses are strengthened or weakened by the manipulation of resultant consequences or effects.

It's like how we teach kids to say 'please' when asking for something. Saying 'please' (an operant response) will result in the likelihood of getting a yes (a manipulated result). The approval, or saying yes when the kid says 'please', is a manipulated consequence. As a result, the child believes that 'please' is the magic word to say if he/she wants to get a 'yes'. If repeated consistently and long enough, that kid will grow up believing that without saying 'please', he/she will never get a 'yes'.

However, we cannot speak of operant conditioning and not mention B.F. Skinner.

Who is B.F. Skinner?

Burrhus Frederic Skinner[3] (1904-1990) was an American psychologist credited with developing the model and principles of operant conditioning. He was raised in Pennsylvania. He majored in English in college but gave up his writing career and turned to psychology a year after graduating. Being a radical behaviourist, he believed that free-will was but an illusion because environmental and genetic influences entirely determined both animal and human behaviour. For research purposes, he worked with rats and pigeons exploring how reinforcement (the environmental consequences) either strengthened or weakened behaviours. He conducted these sorts of experiments in well-monitored and controlled experimental boxes later called the 'Skinner Boxes'. Rumour has it that Skinner raised his daughter in a similar box (a story for another day).

Rats understudy would be deprived of food and water and caged in the Skinner Box. However, if the rat did the required action, such as pressing a button in the cage, a food pellet would be dropped into the food tray. Of course it took a lot of trials to reinforce such a behaviour. But if repeated well enough, the rat would learn to press the button more frequently to earn its food and/or water reward.

So what I mean when I say, put yourself in a Skinner Box is, treat yourself like a lab rat being studied by B.F.Skinner. I want you to manipulate the results of certain actions to either weaken or strengthen the result-producing-actions. The easiest way of doing this is by rewarding yourself for the little acts or advancements you make towards a major desired goal. It is those simple acts that matter and build-up to something significant. It's true what they say; *'the journey of a thousand miles begins with one step'*. And so by taking that one step in the right direction, you have to acknowledge and pat yourself on the back.

By merely asking her out on a date, regardless of whether she agrees or not, you have taken a small step towards enhancing your social life. And that my friend deserves a toast. You only need to start waking up and making it to the gym by 5 a.m. Whether you do the actual lifting of weights or not is a totally different story altogether.

In this experiment, small acts performed by the rats had to be acknowledged. For example, if the rat/pigeon could just get to the corner where the button/lever was located, it would be rewarded with a pellet. The animal would become conditioned to the belief that, *"approaching this corner will get me food."* Through this manipulated reward system, the animal would end up performing the required task to earn more pellets. If continuously conditioned this way, the pigeon/rat would perform amazing feats like pushing the button only when the light is switched on.

Such is what I want for you. To place yourself in a Skinner Box and reward yourself for every simple step you take. It allows those tiny steps to build towards something more significant.

Also in this experiment, Skinner observed that the reinforcement was supposed to be rewarded promptly. The longer the time delay before the reinforcement was given, the weaker it would affect behaviour and vice versa. After acting in a certain desirable way – you should acknowledge it and reinforce that action right away

The strength of operant conditioning through the Skinner Box is that a pellet or reward acts as a reinforcement. Depending on what you seek to achieve, you might employ either a negative or positive reinforcement.

For example, let us say your goal is to become more social – to interact more. Each time you smile or greet a stranger, whether they smile or greet back or not, you need to praise yourself or even tell your friend about it. In return, this small acknowledgement will drive you to continue smiling and greeting people you meet. Your goal, which is to socialize more, will soon be attained. This is an example of Positive Reinforcement in play.

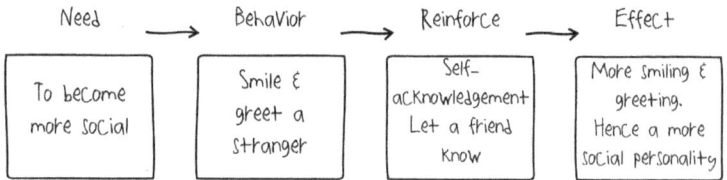

Need	Behavior	Reinforce	Effect
To become more social	Smile & greet a stranger	Self-acknowledgement Let a friend know	More smiling & greeting. Hence a more social personality

Now let us say, your aim is to eliminate foul language from your everyday speech. You then pledge to give/donate ten dollars for every vulgar word you say. In this case, the ten dollars is the reinforcement – but a negative one. Think of it as a punishment instead of a reward.

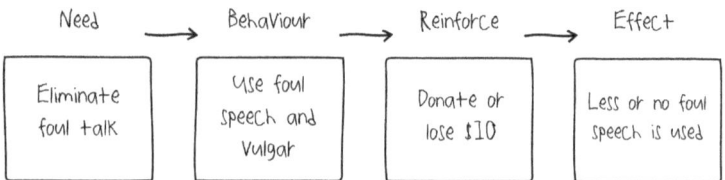

Need	Behaviour	Reinforce	Effect
Eliminate foul talk	Use foul speech and Vulgar	Donate or lose $10	Less or no foul speech is used

For this to work, you will need a serious friend/partner capable of forcefully collecting those ten-dollar penalties.

Speaking of what serious friends or partners can do for you, you can also...

Get yourself an accountability buddy

Unless you are disciplined enough and you have attained self-mastery, staying committed to your plans and goals will be extremely difficult. The urge and tendency to revert to old ways or return into your comfort zone will always be insurmountable.

Even after paying substantial gym subscriptions, many of us would rather lose the money than go work-out at 5 am. Just like how buying books doesn't mean you'll read them. Think about how many times you have purchased healthy foods but later go back to your junk-food diet. How many times have you bought yourself a piggy-bank or opened a savings account but never fully committed to saving?

> *Goals only known to yourself are, most of the time, weak goals and easy to neglect.*

You have often heard that, *"behind every successful man, there is a woman behind him."* Whoever came to that conclusion must have seen men of great stature being influenced by the love of their lives, wives, mistresses, etc. I would like to assume that such men made their plans known to the women in their lives. In other words, the women ended up being these men's accountability buddies who continuously checked on them for progress. And, once the woman became acquainted with the man's intentions, the man had no way of chickening out – unless if he wanted to be seen as a chicken by his partner.

This aforementioned proposition is debatable of course, but in short, all I am saying is sometimes it is better to let someone know your plans. Someone who can push you and force you to act when you feel like quitting. The moment you get that someone in your life, you become unstoppable.

Those who go to the gym can attest to the effectiveness of this method. Working out alone, without someone to push you is not as effective as when you have a gym partner. For you to wake up for those 5 am runs, there has to be someone continually nudging you to stick to your regime plan. It would definitely help if you had someone who understands your plan and body goals. Some even go a step further to investing in a personal body trainer or fitness coach. Even in your life as it is, you might need to hire life-coaches and find mentors who will act as your accountability buddies.

The truth of the matter is that you cannot Become all by yourself. You need to have accountability buddies in various areas of your life to journey along with you. To push you when you feel like quitting, to remind you why you even started in the first place. Isaac Newton was once quoted:

> *"If we have seen far,*
> *It is because we have stood on the*
> *shoulders of giants."*

What he was doing here, was acknowledging his accountability buddies. He was recognizing the people who played or were still playing a part in his inventions and life's journey.

To make sure you get through to the other side, you need to identify your own giants as well. Find those who are willing to let you stand on their shoulders so that you can see farther than you can see right now.

Get yourself an accountability buddy to act as your commitment-partner. If one buddy is not enough, then get many accountability buddies by...

Publicly announce your intentions

Another method to keep you at it is to make a public announcement of your plans. Next time you have a goal to chase, try publishing it for the world to see and notice how committed you will be to attain that goal. There are so many reasons attached to why this method is effective. Saying it in public by default, invites the public to become your accountability buddies. From this public-accountability-buddy-domain, some people want you to realize your goal, and others simply don't care. However, a larger population probably thinks you are not capable of doing it and are waiting to stick it up in your face when you fail. This means you have two good reasons to see your plans through. Firstly, to not let those who believe in you down and secondly, to prove the naysayers wrong.

Having the entire world watch and wait for you to either pass or fail at something can fuel you beyond your imagination. Many of us can testify that the biggest mistake you could make as a teenager was publicizing the boy/girl you liked. If your friends were like mine and they discovered or even just suspected that you liked this certain girl, they would make your life a living hell.

They would make it their job to make sure you confessed your feelings to her. They would set you up to bump into that girl more often and make you uncomfortable in her presence. And, if you failed to confess the feelings you had for her, they would jeer at you for being timid. This is a clear example of what happens when your plans become known by the public. You become compelled to go for it unless you want to be considered timid.

I am super-convinced that whoever designed the wedding ceremony to include the saying out aloud of vows, understood this too. I don't know much about marriages and divorces, however, I am sure that some unions are still standing today because of the vows said in the presence of families and friends. Even those who do go ahead and divorce probably have a hard time trying to forget what they said to each other when they wedded. Undoubtedly, they will recall the promises said, like, *"For better or worse,"* *"Through the bad times,"* or *"Till death do us apart."* It will take a lot to go through with the divorce and pretend the vows were never said. The pledges, oftentimes said in front of friends and family (public), have a way of holding people accountable and forcing them to be committed to the marriage.

Of course, some disregard the promises, but many couples are still together because they told the public that they would be together 'till death' did them apart.

Plans said in public are hard to not go through with. The pressure and expectations will force you to stick to them, and it will not be easy to chicken-out. Otherwise, if we fail, we will be a laughing stock, which is the last thing we want.

Abraham Maslow's[4] hierarchy of needs ranks esteem as one

of the most sought after need by human beings. It comes only second to the need to self-actualize. We are designed to do whatever we can to feed our esteem. Our esteem, in turn, thrives on our achievements, prestige, status, approval, and the respect we get from others. As social animals, we are continually seeking for our peers' admiration and respect. We are programmed to do whatever we can to fit in. We have also learned that to be accepted into certain cliques and groups, we have to behave in a manner that conforms to those groups' standards.

This is what makes announcing our goals in public so effective. Knowing that attaining them will earn us respect from our peers is what will keep us focused. It leaves us with less room to give up. Not doing becomes not an option. So in essence, it means that our desire to be respected could, in effect, propel us go after things we wouldn't have, had we not publicized our intentions.

We want to be seen as people who are committed, go-getters who do not just claim to, but who walk the talk. Our incessant desire to satisfy our esteem can help us through the things we would not have done. The moment our esteem is threatened, and is on the line, we become fueled to do whatever it takes to preserve it.

I tried and tested this technique when I was writing this book. Looking at the task ahead, I feared I was going to quit halfway through it, so announced on social media that I was working on a book. Ever since that post on various social media platforms, I have had countless people pop up from nowhere, asking if the book was ready. If you are reading this, then this technique definitely worked. Believe me when I say, telling the world about what you intend to do has a way of galvanizing you to those plans. I have been pushed towards publishing this book by some people who I don't even know personally.

If you have a major goal that daunts you or that you think you'll quit from pursuing, then I suggest you publicize your intention to get it. This technique also works if you are trying to break bad habits.

Unless you are in a battle – practicing the art of war or planning an attack, only then will publishing your plans be detrimental. But if you are planning to Become, then there is no easier way to keep yourself at it than letting the general public work to your advantage. Let them act as your reminders, motivators, prove-us-wrong-buddies, etc.

Commit irreversibly

Let me tell you a little about myself. I grew up on a farm. My father was and still is a cattle rancher. His business was not that big when he started, so during vacations, my nephew and I would, by default, become cow-herders. We would follow the beasts around the farm all day, ensuring that they didn't jump over to other people's farms and also guarding them against thievery. It was a tedious task, truth be told. We would go deep into the bush with all our necessities in our backpacks only to return home at dusk. We were required to keep the herd feeding in certain designated pastures. Unfortunately, for us to get to these pastures, we had first to cross a river.

The cattle did not seem to have a problem swimming across the river. In fact, they seemed to enjoy it. I, on the other hand, hated swimming across that cold river. So in this situation, we could either swim across the river or walk upstream to a crossing point that was quite a distance away.

We developed a strategy to force us to swim across despite not wanting to. Upon getting there, we would strip ourselves naked, shuffle our clothes into our backpacks and throw the bags across the river. After doing this, we were left with two options; either we would walk upstream stark-naked to the crossing point, or simply swim across to our backpacks. Come to think of it, there wasn't much of choice. The former option was absurd and not feasible on any day.

Most of the time, what keeps us in undesirable places is not because we like it there; it is mostly because of lack of commitment. The reason why we don't follow through with our plans is that we haven't made a huge enough commitment to keep us at it. Even if sometimes we do commit, we leave openings just in case we decide to bail out. We give ourselves ample room to maneuver and wriggle out of it whenever we feel like no longer doing it.

Even though we might actually want it, when the going gets tough, because there is an escape opening, we are prone to use it. We can easily excuse ourselves because, in essence, we didn't sign up for it.

To do the actual 'signing up for it', I suggest that we irreversibly commit to our plans. If you are to Become, to be sure you do it and do it no matter the circumstances, you have to commit to that cause irreversibly. The road to Becoming is yours to create. However,

I urge you to charter a one-way route. Leave no opportunity to do a U-turn and your vehicle does not need review-mirrors. It's an onward journey only. No need to look at what's behind you because it's not like you intend to head in that direction anyway. Right?

A story[5] is told. I have heard and read about it in so many different versions, characters, and details that I still don't know if it happened. Whether it is true or not, its moral remains invaluable to this chapter.

> An army general and his men voyaged across an ocean. He was on a quest to capture and conquer an island. It is said a powerful enemy inhabited this island. It is also understood that the general had suffered heavy casualties during his sail. By the time he reached the island, his army was greatly outnumbered and weakened. Upon disembarking to this island, he ordered his men to burn all the boats they had arrived in. Pure madness, huh? The men complied with this outrageous order. The army general then gave a battle speech in which he told his men that they were left with only two options; conquer or perish.

As you might have guessed, they defeated the powerful enemy and captured the island.

It's easy to retreat when you have an option.
Remove that option, &
Watch how unstoppable you will become.

When I first decided to immerse myself into reading books, I failed dismally at really sticking to it. I downloaded copies of all the great life-changing books by much-appreciated authors. I even got some electronic copies over email, but it didn't work. It was only after I bought a hard copy of Napoleon[6] Hill's *'Think and Grow Rich[7]'* that I actually read a book cover to cover without putting it off for later. Nothing had changed; it was still the same text and the same author. The only element new to this situation was a little commitment I had made to investing and buying the book. Because I had parted ways with my money to buy that book, I felt the need to get something out of it; hence I read it, cover to cover.

What was in play here is what psychologists have termed *'The Sunk Cost Bias[8]'*. The idea is that we are motivated to do some things based on what we have initially invested. It generates an incessant need to continue putting in more effort or investment in the project – so that you can get something out of what you have already put in. This bias also explains how and why sometimes people keep applying themselves to evidently losing ventures. They become so emotionally attached that they will continue pursuing that project despite the reality. Just like in betting – one will keep on placing bets hoping to win on the next round and recover what has already been lost. Sometimes he/she might win it back, but most often, he/she will walk out of that betting house with empty pockets and overdrawn bank accounts.

Once we have put in a considerable investment, then we have managed to commit irreversibly. If we commit or invest something that we value like money, time, etc., then the *Sunk Cost Bias* might work to our advantage. It will help us remain at it because we will be feeling emotionally attached to what we have already put in. Just like how I developed a reading habit because I was buying the books with my hard-earned internship money. That is what we can do for any other task or goal.

The same act of irreversibly committing can be transmuted to almost everything you want to pursue in life. If you find yourself skipping the gym, try this next time; Pay your membership subscription annually. Whenever thoughts of skipping gym invade your mind, make sure you remind yourself of that subscription fee. If that is not enough – rent a gym locker and stock all your work clothes there, you can leave your office keys in that gym locker before heading home every evening. This would mean one way or the other, you now have a big enough reason to head to the gym every morning. This is just another version of committing irreversibly.

The bigger the task, the bigger the required commitment to keep you moving forward. The bigger the commitment made, the bigger the chance of you not-quitting.

This is why I think that the general advice of not putting your eggs in one basket is a bad one. How about you put all our eggs in one basket? Do you think you would let anything happen to that basket? I know for sure that you would guard that basket with your life. Why? Because you have made that huge commitment. A big enough, and irreversible, commitment for that matter. Meaning you have no choice whether you like it or not but to keep your eyes fixated on the basket (for better or worse).

Irreversibly committing can be likened to the burning of a bridge once you cross it. Once it is burnt, there won't be any options left except to proceed forward. If you find yourself not as committed as you need to be, or quitting halfway through, then I urge you to burn the bridges behind you or throw your backpacks to the other side of the river.

Understand the anatomy of motivation

Psychology has a branch of study that seeks to explain the "whys" of behaviour. In other words, it aims to uncover the truth behind motivation. Nevid[9] defined motivation as the *'factors that activate, direct, and sustain goal-directed behaviour'.*

This field of study postulates that we source our motivation from either biological or psychological avenues. Biological sources encapsulate instincts, stimuli, needs, and drives. Whereas incentives, psychosocial needs, and cognitive dissonance constitute the psychological sources of motivation.

Don't worry! I'm not taking you through a psychology lecture. I simply want us to borrow a few aspects from this topic.

We want to keep our motivation levels high, and for us, we need to know the location of a rich motivation well.

Nothing speaks volumes to anyone more than a reward. The benefit attached to a particular goal determines how long we will stay enthralled to it.

Incentives Theory

The *incentives theory*[10] suggests that our perceived value towards goals or objectives determines much of our behaviour and motivation. Usually, before setting a goal, we conduct a cost-benefit analysis to ascertain if it is beneficial for us to pursue.

Before we commit to anything, we first try to answer the question, "is it worth it?" And if we can't find a strong enough reason, we will automatically disengage.

If we incentivise our plans, goals, and dreams well enough, our motivation levels will always remain high. We ought to redefine 'why we are doing what we are doing', and the definition should be that which gives us an extra boost to keep at it. The easiest way to do it is to attach clear and huge benefits or incentives to the goal.

You've often seen people behave differently when facing the same encounter. When two people fail at something in a similar fashion, one quits while the other perseveres. Why? Simply because they incentivised whatever they were pursuing differently. To one person, a gym is a place of excruciating pain and harsh early morning runs. To another, it is a place to create a healthy body, long life, and reduce stress levels. Now, who do you think between those two will visit the gym more frequently?

Another story is told.

Three men working for a construction company were asked what they did for a living. This is how they responded:

The first one: 'I lay bricks.'

The second one: 'I construct buildings.'

The third one: 'I build the world.'

You can imagine which of the above three woke up every day with a huge smiley-face, feeling energized to take the day head-on at the construction site.

Incentivising our goals keeps us at it. Visualizing the trophy to be won will help us keep our eyes locked on the ball - always. Look at it this way: if you are dead scared to ask that girl out, next time you see her tell yourself something like, *"this is my chance to talk to my future-wife."* If the incentive becomes big enough, then you will be compelled to go for it, no matter what comes your way. Whatever you seek out to achieve, please make yourself aware of all the benefits attached to it. It's even better if you create your personal metaphoric benefits. Instead of thinking of yourself as someone who just lays bricks – see yourself as someone who is building the world.

We only start procrastinating on our plans when the incentives start becoming unclear. When, for some reason, we begin revaluing the benefit to a lower value than it initially was we start doubting the worthiness of our goals. This is how we become reluctant about something that at first enthused us.

When we first set out on a quest to get this or that, we were excited, overflowing with energy, and oozing with confidence. But somehow, when we looked up the long road ahead of us, our energy level instantaneously dropped. Most often this is because we started focusing on the work at hand and immediately downsized the benefit or reward that was to be gained.

I advise that we hold the vision or reward dear always, and it better be a big enough reward. The incentive to be gained is the fuel you need to make it through. Imagine how it would be like to Become. Envision how the victory would look like, what it would mean to you have that body, speak on that platform, publish that book, date that person, have that job, etc.

To be honest, without a significant and clear enough incentive, you stand little chance of persevering all the way to the end.

Cognitive Dissonance Theory

Cognitive Dissonance Theory[11] has it that people derive motivation from the need to align behaviours to their attitudes or beliefs. While it can be a source of motivation, I want us to look at how, through cognitive dissonance, we can model our lives to get us the objects of our desires.

Let's say you are an alcoholic. Let us also assume you are disgusted by it, and you are aware that overindulging in this activity literally erodes your life and ruins your relationships with your loved ones. You are in a state of internal conflict because your beliefs and behaviours are out of sync. You find yourself overdrinking, but you also believe it to be harmful to yourself and those around you. That internal conflict is what they call *cognitive dissonance.* It's an unpleasant feeling and in a situation like this, the human tendency is to try to reduce this dissonance.

We do whatever we can to reduce this discrepancy between our belief system and our behaviours.

There are four ways of achieving this;
1. We can change the belief
2. We can change the behaviour
3. We can justify our atrocious behaviour
4. We can simply ignore

If our attitudes or beliefs are out of sync with our behaviours and habits, then we will find ourselves in an unpleasant state. This means that we can use our internal system as a compass. Whenever we head in a direction we are not supposed to, that inner compass can notify us. If we listen closely and attentively enough, through cognitive dissonance, we can tell if we are where we are supposed to be and doing what we are supposed to be doing with who we are supposed to be doing it with. So much of Becoming has to do with harmoniously aligning our belief system to our actions.

Once we have deduced what we believe in and mapped out our plan of action, we can always pay attention to that internal system. Any misalignment will be shown to us through the existence of a dissonance.

To put our two theories (*Incentive & Cognitive*) into perspective let us look at this example:

Let's assume that this time around, you are a chronic smoker. You are literally huffing and puffing your life away in smoke. A medical report has revealed that at this rate, you should expect a visit from the Grim Reaper very soon. You initially decide that you want to quit smoking because the idea of dying doesn't sit well with you. On your quest to quit smoking, you can incentivise it. In this case, the incentive is a little more time on earth, so you can visit the Egyptian Pyramids or do whatever you yearn for before you die. You are likely to really take quitting smoking more seriously because the incentive placed on this goal is huge – your life is on the line here *(Incentive Theory)*.

Also, because what you now believe in is not matching what you are doing, that is, living longer vs. smoking which is killing you, this discrepancy creates a conflicted internal state *(Cognitive Dissonance)*.

In an effort to reduce this dissonance you either:

1. Change your behaviour

You can quit smoking right away.

2. Change your belief

You can tell yourself, *"Smoking is not that bad – it doesn't kill."*

3. Justify your behaviour

Smoking helps soothe my nerves, de-stress, relax, etc., or

4. You can choose just to ignore

Whatever! It is what it is. We are all going to die anyway.

By first incentivising what we are pursuing and secondly, matching our beliefs to our behaviours, we can basically achieve anything. If you believe that smoking is killing you, then you will put in enough effort to quit it. And each time you find yourself smoking again and justifying it or trying to ignore it, it means you don't believe it deeply enough. It also means you haven't given yourself a good enough reason.

This is exactly what happens with most, if not all, of our plans in life. Incentives and Cognitive Dissonance theories play a significant role in dictating whether we go through with it or not. Now that we have uncovered it, we can easily Become because we can use psychological sources of motivation to our benefit. We have now become conscious of the internal radar within us so we can pursue our goal relentlessly with so much drive. The drive that we can create through incentivising and matching our beliefs to our attitudes. Becoming has now been made easy. If we attach valuable enough incentives and align our beliefs and attitudes, Becoming becomes a thrilling joyride.

Manipulate the Action Loop

As we have seen, action and motivation are best buddies. We now know that what prompts us to act is motivation. Whether it is a pull or push motivation, it will always get us to work. However, we also established at the beginning of this chapter that motivation itself could sometimes run out. And, if we are not careful, we will end up putting our entire plans in jeopardy.

But is it always the case that, once our motivation falters, we are done, and we can't move? I am sure you have once heard yourself saying something like, "I can't do it right now – I just don't feel like it." Without motivation, we cannot act, so we think. We believe that we can only do it when we are motivated. We are under the impression that we have to feel like doing it in order for us to actually do it.

When we don't have a sense of inspiration within, we then resort to procrastinating. We know what we should be doing, but we believe we can't do it right now. "Maybe later, once we are motivated again", we reckon.

This what procrastination is; delaying or putting off for later or even never, what you should be doing now. It's staying in bed a little longer, even after the alarm sounds. It's sitting on that couch – movie bingeing, eating chips at the expense of that assignment or project.

If this is you, if you believe you aren't doing what you ought to be doing because you are not motivated to do so, then I want to introduce you to the 'Action Loop.'

Motivation indeed breeds action. If you are motivated well enough – you will definitely act. Like this:

$$Motivation$$

$$\downarrow$$

$$Action$$

As long as we are motivated, it's easy to do or be anything. Without this motivation, we think, and we doubt we can do anything. However, this is only partially true and here is why:

Have you ever found yourself low on motivation, and feeling as if you can't do something you are supposed to? And then, with that ounce of motivation, you decide to act anyway. Remember how it sucked the life out of you at first? But as you progressed, you found yourself more motivated than when you started. The more you focused on it, the more you felt a little more motivated to continue. I am certain you have managed to start doing something without much zeal, but you ended up doing it for hours. It is not a false then, to posit that action also breeds motivation. Action and motivation reciprocate to create what I will call an Action Loop. This is a continuous process whereby if you are motivated, you act. When you act, you become more motivated, and thus you continue acting. This never-ending loop can start from either motivation or action; whichever way you start, it gets things done.

Motivation

Action

Nike[12] tells us about this loop when it says, *"Just Do It."* Nike is saying I don't care if it's a good time or a bad time; I don't care if you feel like doing it or not − *"Just Do it."* Because by just doing it, whether you feel like it or not, you will end up feeling inspired and entranced with the task at hand. Just do it because action breeds motivation, and motivation breeds more action, and on and on.

The irony in this is, as I write this, it is exactly 10:04 p.m. I had quite a tiresome day packed with many meetings. I had decided to put off writing for tomorrow so that I can rest. However, I decided to quickly review the previous chapter before I went to bed. It's funny how it has been 3 hours since I started that reviewing process. When I started, I was low on motivation, and I had no intention of writing but now I have been writing for hours. That is what the *action loop* does. Even if you don't feel like it, if you just start doing it - you'll end up doing it like you initially wanted to.

If you have tried writing an essay or business proposal − you'll agree that often the first sentence is like a climb up Mt Everest with a backpack full of sand. But, once you start writing, you soon get into the groove. The action loop requires you to conquer inertia. Just start and let momentum take care of the rest. It's like the morning alarm situation. No one ever feels delighted to get out of bed, but if you intend to beat the snooze urge, you have to jump out of bed before even thinking about it. That action will breed the motivation to stay out of bed and get ready for the day. In that same light, the easiest way to have a cold shower in the morning is to jump into it, without giving much thought about it.

The next time you feel uninspired to act, try doing it for at least five solid minutes and see how far you will go from:

Demotivated >> Action >> Motivated >> More Action >> More Motivation >> More and More Action>> More and More Motivation ...

The journey to Becoming is never going to be sweet, many times you won't feel as inspired as you would hope to be. But, this should not bring you to a halt because by just acting, you'll fill up your motivation tank.

Chapter Summary

To avoid not doing

---

1. Put yourself in a Skinner Box.

Reward yourself for every step you take in the direction you intend to go. (baby steps count too)

2. Get yourself an accountability buddy.

Find someone who will push you and hold you accountable when you don't act as you intended.

3. Publicly Announce Your Intentions.

Make your intentions known to everyone (they will collectively act as your accountability buddies.

4. Commit Irreversibly.

Give yourself a 'No Way Out.'

5. Understand the Psychology behind Motivation.

(Incentive Theory & Cognitive Dissonance Theory)
Incentivise your efforts and align your beliefs to your actions.

6. Use the Action Loop.

Act despite feeling motivated or not.
Motivation induces action and action breeds motivation as well.

CHAPTER FIVE

THE HARSH REALITY

'If death is inevitable, one should try to die well.'

- Mary Jo Putney

In June 2018, I perhaps had one of the most unpleasant awakening moments of my life. I lost my dear aunt, Rosemary, to an accident. If I were to describe Rosemary to you with one word, I would say 'awesome'. She was one of those relatives you would want to spend as much time with as possible. She was also an adamant Christian and a well-loved person in her community as she contributed so considerably through her time and resources. In fact, the accident that took her life was a journey dedicated to church-related matters. The car which was being driven by her church pastor, went out of control, overturned, and she died on the spot. Just like that, a sudden and unexpected accident had cut her life short, leaving behind her two sons and a loving husband. She had just opened her restaurant, a beauty parlor, and had also ventured into horticulture projects on her farm, only to mention a few. The untimeliness of her death left so many heartbroken and confused.

The passing of my aunt had so many effects on my way of thinking. Apart from the pain, her death had a profound impact on how I viewed life; my perspective was shifted abruptly.

What you already know and should know again

Only one thing in this entire universe is evidently certain. We can argue all day on other matters pertaining to politics, religion, health, science, everything else, but death. It's something we already know, but we rarely face this *harsh reality* squarely.

As a human species, we dread the idea that one day we are going to depart from this life form and probably be forgotten. In fact, the fear of death is ranked amongst the top six underlying human fears. However, it is inescapable and inevitable, and as cold as it sounds, WE ARE ALL GOING TO DIE.

What makes it worse is the fact that death comes as an uninvited guest. No notice – No heads-up, nothing of the sort. My aunt's death taught me a myriad of valuable lessons, including that death was unpredictable and uncalled for. Death just happens, whether you deserve it or not (I wonder if there's anyone who deserves to die anyway). Death doesn't have a selection criteria list when choosing its victims. No matter how good or bad you are, no matter how many plans or unfinished projects you are still pursuing, the Grim Reaper will knock on your door at any day. Death doesn't care or acknowledge life expectancies, health, financial status, or fame. It just happens, and it will remain that way. Death remains a mystery, and its selection is so randomized that even the world's geniuses have failed to come up with a formula to calculate one's date of death.

This is the *harsh reality*. That we are all going to die, and we do not know how, when, where, and even worse - why! We're simply going to die. Full stop! As if this is enough, upon passing on, we'll definitely have a good week on social media with people mourning us through statuses, sorry captions, and sad hashtags, but sooner or later, people will somehow carry on with their lives.

I am not saying all this to sound somber. On the contrary, I want us to use this *harsh reality* to work to our advantage. Consider this just a nudge designed to wake you up.

The mind-boggling questions I would then throw at you would be: since we are all going to die one way or another – what are you doing with your life? Is what you are doing going to give you satisfaction when you draw your last breath? If you die today, what would you be remembered for? If we are all going to die, does it matter whether or not your plans and business ventures sucked?

You see, in the blink of an eye, your entire life could just go poof (disappear) just like that. It could be in the next thirty years, two or three months, or even tomorrow. You could die at work, in the shower, in your sleep, or choke on your favorite pie. You could die in the most bizarre way thinkable. If you have ever watched the movie called Final Destination[1], you'll understand what I mean. No one can and ever will do anything about this *harsh reality*.

Funnily enough, as I write this, the entire globe is trembling at the wrath of possibly the deadliest pandemic of our generation. The Coronavirus[2] (COVID 19) pandemic has brought the world to a halt. Economies, businesses, dreams, and personal plans have all been shattered by something no one anticipated. But what makes it worse is the number of people who have died since COVID 19 was declared a global pandemic by the World Health Organisation[3.] Over a million people have died to date, and we're still counting. Such is the unprecedented and sad times we find ourselves in.

Now, think about the people whose lives have been cut short but also had plans for tomorrow, next month and next year. But death did what it does best, coming in as an uninvited guest. No one knows what is looming in the future. I consider it a privilege to be able to be writing this book right now and you should consider yourself blessed too, to be reading it. Many people had planned to write their books as well, but they are on respiratory ventilators fighting for their lives.

Hear me out: I am proposing that we make peace with this reality. The reality that our breathing is metered, and without notice, one day, we will be gasping for air.

This being a reality, I would like to suggest that, before you die (which is definite), at least make sure you have lived first. Instead of fretting and stressing over something this certain, I am here to offer an alternative; *"Let us live first before we die."*

Life is ridiculously and unpredictably short to not live it fully.

The very fact that we are all going to die should, in actuality, be the motivation we need to do what we think we were designed to do. It should be the reason we try at anything we love and value because hey, we're all dying soon, remember? This is why I am supporting the notion that before we die, we live first. In other words, before we die, let us Become first.

Believe it or not, not all of us are living. There is a huge difference between living and merely existing. When I say 'let us live', I am calling upon you not just to survive. Enough of existing, surviving, and breathing, – it's time to thrive. You have to. You deserve to. You ought to.

The fact that you're reading this book tells me something about you. You are not satisfied by only surviving, you also yearn to thrive, and that is a good starting point, wanting!

I once heard someone say that, *"we live for the dash."*

Yes! The dash.

He argued that only two dates where fixed in every person's life:

1. Date of birth, and

2. Date of death.

On your tombstone, there will be those two dates (both of which you have zero control over). These two dates will be separated by a dash (-). That dash symbolizes your entire life and all your accomplishments. The power is in each and every one of us to design the dash (-) between these two dates. It remains our choice to either unleash ourselves on the world as we live in the dash moment. Or, we can allow the date after the dash (date of death) to cripple us as we fear its occurrence. The dash is where all the action is.

People who have understood the randomness and unexpectedness of death concentrate on creating spectacular dashes. You have to understand that you can only Become in the dash period. You cannot Become before your birth, and you certainly cannot Become after you die. You owe it to yourself then, to make this your most important project – to design and color that dash as awesomely as you believe it should be.

After all, even if you fail at it, will it really matter, considering that you are going to die? And, to make it even better, everyone else is also going to die.

The younger and groovy generation seem to have understood the harsh reality – that we are all going to die. They actually created an acronym for it – YOLO, 'You Only Live Once.' The only problem with this is that it is used to justify living recklessly and without any consideration. For a teenager, living fully oftentimes encapsulates following the trends, booze and drugs, accompanied by lots of sex. YOLO is about not worrying about the consequences because well, you only have one life.

I find it an oxymoron that they know that they only have one life, yet they choose to live recklessly. Wouldn't it make more sense to live a life with meaning? If you are one of those who perceive 'YOLO' in this way, then I would like to urge you to redefine what life really is.

To be honest, in the grandest scheme of things living recklessly and justifying it by YOLO, is not the way to go. We should never forget that unlike a cat, we humans don't have nine lives, we only have one. And, this one life we have is the one we agreed earlier to be unpredictably short. For that reason, we should constantly remind ourselves that our clocks are ticking. *If We Are To Become*, the YOLO mantra is necessary. Only if we use it to drive us to live meaningful lives. It should force us to get our lives on track and never look back.

> *We should never be scared of dying.*
> *The only thing that should scare us,*
> *however, is not living*

In his book, *Reasons To Stay Alive*[4], Matt Haig said something that hit the bull's eye. He said, *"I find that being grimly aware of the mortality can make me steadfastly determined to enjoy life where life can be enjoyed. It makes me value precious moments with my children, and with the woman I love. It adds intensity in bad ways, but also good ways".*

What is the value of life?

When we start asking ourselves questions pertaining the value of life, then we know that we are on the right track. This is perhaps but a question that, if properly answered, would greatly assist humankind. Knowing what really gives my life or your own life, infinite value is important.

There was once a father who had a mute son. The son, due to his inability to speak, was angry at life and often depressed. He couldn't find meaning in his life, let alone a reason to ever be alive. He viewed himself as someone disadvantaged through this disability. One day, on the verge of giving up on life, he asked his father what the value of life was. The father instead gave his son a shiny colorful rock and gave him a task. He told him to go to the market and try to sell the stone. He further advised him that whenever a prospective buyer asked for the stone's price, all he had to do was raise two fingers and sell for whatever fee the buyer gave him.

Sure enough, at the market came along a lady who inquired about the stone's price, and as advised, the boy raised his two fingers – the lady delightedly paid him two coins and left with the stone. The following day, the father gave his son another identical stone and advised him to follow yesterday's procedure but now selling at the local museum stand. This time around a tourist came along, and after the boy showed him two fingers – he paid two hundred coins and happily left. Baffled by this experience, the boy ran back home.

The father urged him to approach a rare stone collector's shop and try the same procedure. Upon inspecting the rock, the collector asked for the price, and again the boy raised two fingers. The collector, in turn, paid him a hefty fee of two hundred thousand coins.

The father explained to his son that the value of his life was like the value of the rock. It was determined by the environment he put himself in and in whose hands he would place himself in.

In the market, to a random lady, a rock could be worth two coins. In a museum in the hands of a tourist, it could score two hundred coins, whereas to a knowledgeable stone collector, that same stone could be worth even more.

This one short life you have could be so valuable, and it could also be valueless. You need to monitor the environment you place yourself in. Ask yourself if you're not in a market when you supposed to be in a stone collectors shop. The environment you place yourself will either increase or lower your value. Strive to be in places that value you or at least make sure you are where your value is being increased.

This same principle applies to the people you place around yourself. Not everyone will see how valuable you are. The problem with most of us is that we expect the wrong people to be valuing us. The key to happiness is placing yourself amongst those that appreciate your skills and talents. Be around those who value you as a person. You cannot expect a blacksmith to find you valuable when you are a typist. Knowing that not everyone and not every environment will value you as much as you actually are should free you from expecting value recognition from wrong people and places.

To Become, we will have to find the environments and people that are in need of our skills and abilities. This is why, for every business plan – market research is necessary. All market research is, is looking for places and people that will buy our product. Such you should do with your life too, know where you are valued and who wants you.

Keep this story at the back of your head as you journey along this self-improvement journey:

> A COCK was once strutting up and down the farmyard among the hens when suddenly he espied something shining amid the straw. "Ho! Ho!" quoth he, "that's for me," and soon rooted it out from beneath the straw. What did it turn out to be but a Pearl that, by some chance, had been lost in the yard. You may be a treasure," quoth Master Cock, "to men that prize you, but for me, I would rather have a single barley-corn than a peck of pearls."
>
> –Aesop's Fable[5]

You are no different from the pearl in this story. If you put yourself in a barn, then your chances of appreciating in value are very slim. If you expect to be recognized as valuable by roosters, then you are in for a treat because roosters would rather have corn than pearls.

You are priceless! You matter! You are valuable!
The only problem is,
You are in the wrong environment &
You are expecting value recognition from the wrong people.
Change the people around you, your environment, or both,
And, watch as your value skyrockets

The Japanese's way is the way

Did I say life was unpredictably short? What if I were to tell you that there is a way to subvert this assertion? Ancient Japan has had it all along. They have always had the formula that human beings continuously seek, and they call it Ikigai[6] - the reason for being. It is suspected that Ikigai is the reason for the longevity of life in Japan.

In 1995, a research[7] was carried out in Japan to investigate the connection between having a 'life worth living' (*Ikigai*) and the all-cause mortality. All-cause mortality being, all of the deaths that occur in a population, regardless of the cause. The Ohkasi Study, as they referred it to, initially involved the studying of 51,218 Japanese adults. However, the final analysis was limited to 43,391 subjects (20,625 men and 22,766 women).

When asked, if they had *Ikigai* in their lives'? 59% (25,596) claimed they did, 36.4% (15,782) were uncertain, and 4.6% (2,013) didn't have it.

For a period of seven years, follow up studies were conducted on these subjects. At the end of the study period (31 December 2001), 7% of the subjects (3,048) had died, and 12% (5,187) had been lost during follow-ups.

Of the 3,048 deaths, 1,100 were from cancer, 971 deaths had resulted from Cardiovascular Diseases (mainly stroke), 241 from pneumonia, and 186 from external causes.

These numbers are far from what's fascinating. The results from this study showed that, unlike those who had found their *Ikigai*, those who hadn't were more likely to be unemployed, unmarried, and have poor self-rated health. They were also found to have lower educational achievements, high stress, severe body pains, limited physical functionality, and be less likely to walk. It was also found that those who hadn't found a sense of Ikigai had an increased risk of all-cause mortality. In simple terms, those without a sense of *Ikigai* were more prone to death.

The study also showed that those who had no sense of Ikigai had a significantly higher chance to be suffering from cardiovascular related diseases. Remember the 186 deaths resulting from external causes? 90 of the 186 were suicide related cases, and upon taking a closer look, it was discovered that those without Ikigai significantly constituted this group.

However, upon further examination, no correlation was found between lack of *Ikigai* and deaths associated with cancer and pneumonia. Which of course makes sense. Whether or not you have a sense of *Ikigai*, it does not exempt you from the exposure of carcinogens that cause cancer or the lung infections that cause pneumonia. Whether you have Ikigai or not, cancer and/

or pneumonia can equally take your life. In a nutshell, this study concluded that those who didn't have a sense of Ikigai were more likely to have both a poorer socioeconomic and objective health status.

The origin of the word *Ikigai* goes back to the Heian period (794-1185). It's a combination of two words; 'iki' which translates to life and 'gai' which describes 'value' or worth.'

The ancient wise philosophers of Japan argued that to find value, joy, or worth in your life; you had to satisfy four crucial areas by:

1. Doing what you are good at

2. Doing what the world needs

3. Doing what you can get paid for

4. Doing what you love

The idea is that, whatever undertaking you invest your time in should try to feed one if not all of those four sectors.

Through the Ikigai model, something you are both 'good at' and you 'love doing' defines your passion/s.

Your life's mission is made up of what you 'love doing' and what the 'world needs.'

The profession you choose to pursue should be born out of what you are 'good at' and what you can 'get paid for.'

Finally, your vocation should be guided by obviously what the 'world needs' and what you can 'get paid for.'

Like this:

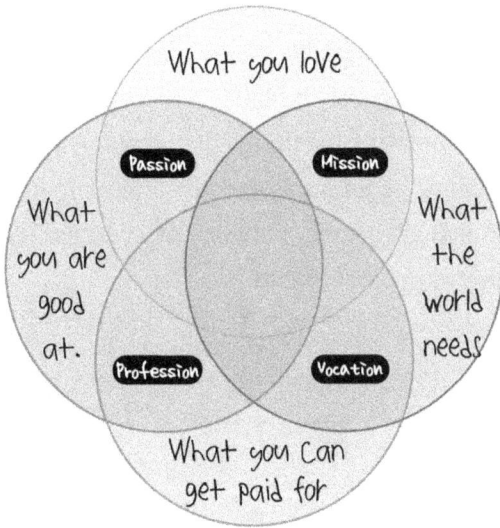

It is prudent to have a clearly defined passion, profession, vocation, and mission. When you intersect your profession, vocation, mission, and passion, you finally attain Ikigai. When you have managed to link up what you do to satisfy these four areas then, your reason for being will become apparent. To Become and to increase your value and sense of self-worth, make sure you find what you are passionate about, define your mission and make it your profession and vocation.

To make you fully understand why these four pillars are necessary and inalienable, let us consider what happens if you decide to neglect one pillar.

Doing what you are not good at.

If you are not 'good at what you do', then according to the *Ikigai* model you will not be a professional and neither will you be able to find passion in what you do. Stay with me on this one. See, if you are not competent, then it is fair to say that you are not a professional. You can only be called a professional at something if you are good at that something. Also, keeping in mind that the ingredients of any passion are pure love and competence (despite the proportions). This then nullifies any chance of developing a passion if there is a lack of expertise.

> *It's not enough to love it without being good at it.*

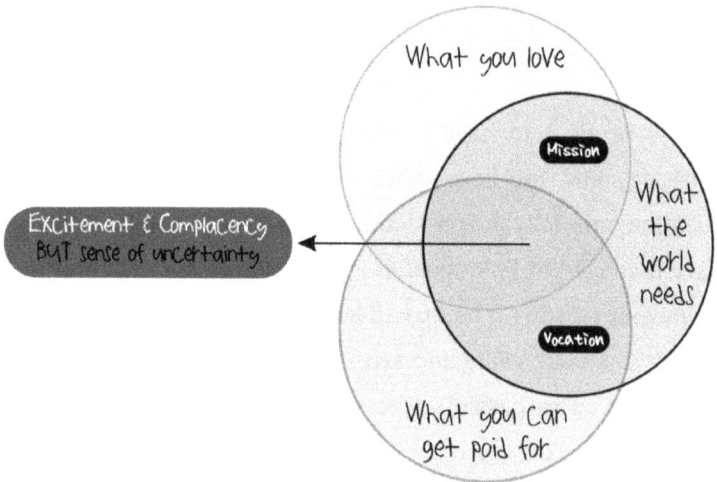

Without competence, you'll only attain a vocation and a mission, and with these two, you are guaranteed to live quite an exciting life. Doing what the world needs, which also happens to be what you love and getting paid for it in the process - sure is fascinating. The downside of this scenario is that it breeds complacency and a sense of uncertainty. The reason for this is that if competence doesn't matter, why would you go out of your way to upgrade your knowledge and skillset? And, since you are not the best at what you do, you remain dispensable and easily replaceable once a competent person passes by.

As we live in a highly competitive world, you cannot afford to be not-good at what you do. To remove all job insecurities and uncertainties, you've got to make sure you are really good at what you do. If you are not, then set out to today to improve your competence level.

Doing nothing that serves the world.

When you decide to trudge through life without considering what the world needs from you, you will miss out on having a vocation. Secondly, without doing what the world needs, you will eliminate any possibility of having a mission.

If your life's mission lacks the element of what the world needs, then I am afraid what you call a mission is not a mission. I doubt if the term mission should be attached to what you claim to have.

> *A mission that does not serve the world is not a mission.*

I am sure you have often heard about people who went through life living only for themselves and their personal motives. Usually, these type of stories predictably end with those people lacking fulfilment, being isolated, and probably feeling useless. The satisfaction that emanates from a situation whereby you are doing something you love, you happen to be quite good at, and getting paid for it, might be tempting to pursue. But failure to do something for the world leads to the lack of a much-sought after fulfilment. This is also in-line with what people call midlife crisis – when you are halfway through life, and you realize how starved your inner-being is.

Without servicing the world, you might reap satisfaction from what you do but oftentimes you'll be left feeling useless.

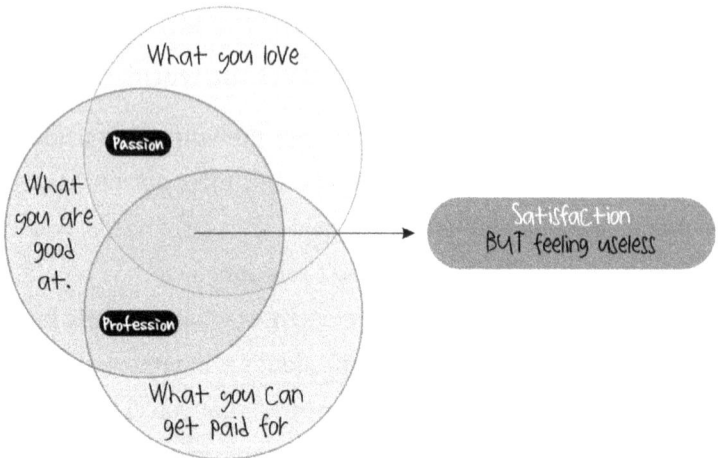

Some argue that serving the world should be what we focus on in our lives – setting it as the foundation of everything else we do and letting the other areas to flourish as by-products. I don't know about that but, what I do know is whether your service to the world is a primary or a secondary obligation, both cases will reward you with a mission and vocation.

Doing what you can't get paid for.

I certainly hope I am not the only one who has met people who believe that money is not necessary in life. You'd be surprised by the number of people out there who shun other people for making money. Usually, the 'holier-than-thou' friends of ours spread the message that money is evil. People pursuing money are often made out to be cunning, selfish, bad people etc. Through this conditioning, many are left despising anyone with money-making motives. In a way, society applauds for and celebrates those in poverty. Look around you, and you'll notice how those in low places are often viewed as somehow noble and saintly whilst those with money are considered to be evil charlatans.

The truth of the matter is we live in a capitalist world and it is no secret that money is important. Having money will give you the freedom you need to live your dreams, feed and clothe yourself, support your loved ones and those in need.

> *Having a lot of money won't make you happy Having little/or no money won't make you happy either. So why not have it?*

If you are not getting paid for what you do, then you won't have a profession nor a vocation. It admittedly sounds noble to neglect money and financial rewards in place of doing what you love, which you happen to be good at and serves the world all at once. It is delightful, and a sense of fullness can be cultivated, but you will be broke and be lacking of financial freedom.

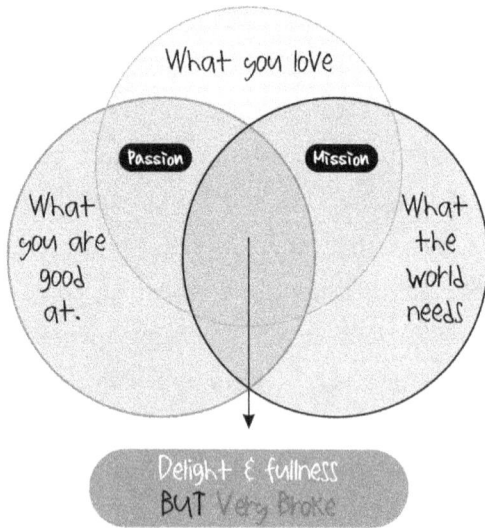

Neglecting what you love.

Can I ask you something? Why are you doing it if you don't love it? If it does not feed your soul – then why are you still at it? Having agreed that this one life we have is incredibly short – does it make sense to waste it away doing what you don't love?

I am saddened by people who go through their short lives neglecting their desires in the hope of not being called selfish. I believe this is the one area that you can be justified of being selfish. When it comes to what you love, you deserve to be selfish (in a healthy way of course). *If You Are To Become*, you have to have love for that which you are doing. Without an appreciation for what you're doing, there is little room to guarantee real genuine success.

People who do what they love, stick to it no matter how tough the going gets. Love will always fuel one to pursue ambitions at whatever cost. Usually, those without love for what they are doing easily quit, end up succumbing to pressure and cut corners.

> *You only have one short life. One way to easily waste it is to do something you don't have love for.*

By doing something you don't love, you automatically refute your passion and your mission. Many people are caught in this dilemma where they are doing something they are good at, getting paid and also serving the world. These are the people who seem to have it all but are always complaining about feeling empty. Reason being, they surely are good at what they do, which serves the world and the world pays for it – they live comfortably, but

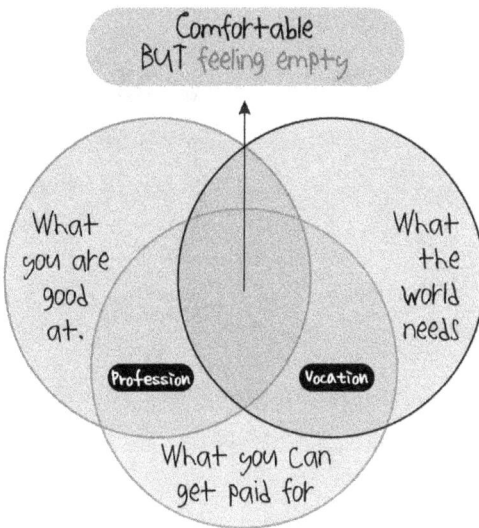

there remains an unfillable void in their life. Lack of passion and mission always starves the soul.

I can't stress this enough, make sure you do what you love or you love what you do – whichever way, there has to be some form of love. James Clear[8] put it succinctly when he said, '*Just for a moment, ignore what you have been taught. Ignore what society has told you. Ignore what others expect of you. Look inside of yourself and ask, "What feels natural to me? When have I felt alive? When have I felt like the real me?" No internal judgments or people-pleasing. No second-guessing or self-criticism. Just feelings of engagement and enjoyment. Whenever you feel authentic and genuine, you are headed in the right direction.'*

Ikigai
A JAPANESE CONCEPT MEANING A REASON FOR BEING

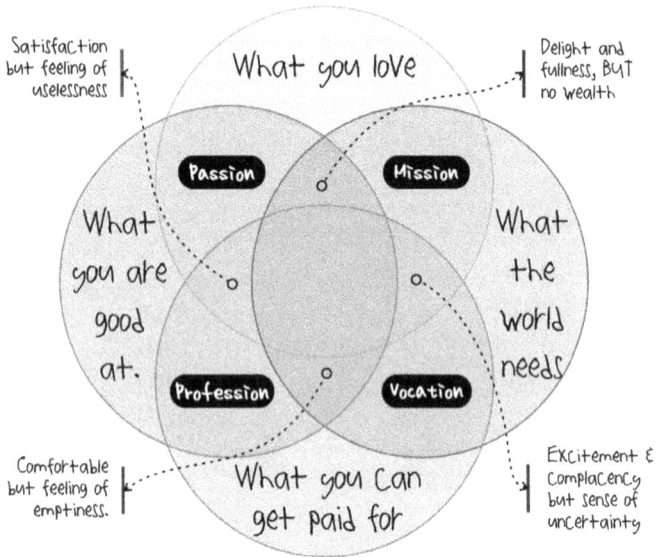

Please don't do this. Please!

Allow me to make two assumptions: firstly, I am going to assume that by now, as you are reading this, you have in your mind what it means to live meaningfully. Secondly, you are driven and ready to live that meaningful life; in other words, you are ready to Become.

Having made these assumptions – I want to expose a common mistake that most of us make in life. A mistake that often impedes us from Becoming. It will hopefully enlighten us as to why the life we were designed for seems to be elusive. This is a 'Don't Do' for someone striving to Become.

Have you ever stopped to see how many of us die trying to be someone else? We get so worked up trying to live like someone else at the expense of our true self. We look at people who live or lived a life that seemingly resonates with us and basically decide we are going to be the 'next' them. It is very true what Schopenhauer[9] said; *"We forfeit three-fourths of ourselves in order to be like other people."* It explains why we read books on biographies and why we listen to talks given by other people until we know them more than ourselves.

Hold your guns!

I also read books and biographies, I listen to speakers, and I look up to some people as well. And you should too. There is nothing wrong with that, trust me.

But I am talking about those who, in Schopenhauers' words,

forfeit themselves to be like other people. Those of us who believe that living like somebody else is plausible. People who end up neglecting the desires of their innermost selves trying to imitate others.

We have become gullible as a human species. We are in search of *'Life's Templates'*, and we are being sold on to schemes, courses, books etc. All because they are said to have an answer towards life, a short cut, a key to happiness etc. Freethinkers at this very moment in time are very rare to come across in this world.

> *We are neglecting who we are, for who others are.*

Factually speaking, you are one of a kind. There is only one you in this universe and no one can ever be you. If that is true, then you will also never be someone else. If you accept this as the truth, then why do you waste your time trying to live somebody else's life - when all that you will ever be, is a just second to the original?

I want you to view it like this: life is like a talent show such as "America's Got Talent[10]" or "X-Factor[11]". The world itself can be thought of as a stage. You only get one shot at it — one chance to impress the judges and the audience. The bizarre and rather unfortunate part is, no one gets to rehearse their act. As soon as you get onto the stage, your time starts ticking. Some get to stay on stage longer than others (you have no say in that). You cannot pause, rewind or fast-forward your time on stage.

All of us have been in the audience before, and we have watched and cheered other performers. We have dreamed and imagined ourselves getting a similar heartwarming standing ovation and receiving awards on this stage. When our name is finally called, we are somehow deluded. We are under the impression that trying that act that won people's hearts before will have the same effect this time around. In simpler terms, we try to copy somebody's moves from A to Z, and when we do this, we oftentimes get booed off the stage and wish the stage would just swallow us.

If you decide to glide over the stage moonwalking like Michael Jackson[12], then that's it. You will not get to showcase your own original act. The audience will not even be drawn to your act because well, they have seen it before. It was, by the way, more captivating initially seeing it from MJ himself. Even if you were to do it better than MJ, it won't change the fact that they are MJ's moves.

The saddest part is, with this kind of approach, we never get a chance to showcase our own original talent on the stage of life. What makes it more painful is most of us will realize how not worth it, it was, to role play, but unfortunately our time on stage would have run out.

The former United States of America's First Lady, Michelle Obama[13] once said in her graduation commencement speech, *"success is not about how your life looks to others; it's about how it feels to you. Being successful is not about being impressive – it's about being inspired (and, that's what it means to be your true self). It means looking inside of yourself and being honest about what you truly enjoy doing because graduates I can promise you, you will never be happy plodding through someone's idea of success. Success is only meaningful and enjoyable if it feels like your own"*

They say the wealthiest place in the world is the graveyard and I do not doubt that even for a second. People die without using their talents, without bringing forth their ideas because they were busy living some other people's lives. How sad? In Michelle's words – *they spent their lives busy plodding through someone's idea of success.*

It's better to be authentic in your walk no matter how awful you think it is, than to be perfect walking like someone else. Because hey, look, if you do the latter, you'll get disqualified and dragged off-stage and if you do the former, you will at least have a shot. You never know, the world might like and appreciate it (or maybe not). But what's important is, it will be your own walk. You'll get a chance to be stared at, at least. I mean, it is better to lose doing something authentic and what you love, than fail at doing something you hate and is inauthentic to you – that would be a double slap.

We wake up daily listening to podcasts of what other people think we should do. We read their books. We follow them on social media. When was the last time you listened to your inner voice? When was the last time you took an introspection to check your inner compass, if whether or not you were still headed towards your north star?

Research has shown that there is an undeniable correlation between depression and heavy social media indulgence. Some researchers have termed it Facebook Overload[14]. It has been noted, especially in young adults. It is suggested that, those that spend more time on social media tend to show more signs of depression. The reason being obvious; the individuals immersed in social media tend to have a falsified view of what the world is really like. The metrics of success they adopt, what they perceive to be socially acceptable and the standards of being are all in one way or another biased.

Everyone on Facebook, Instagram, and Twitter etc. seems to be making it in life. Success is celebrated more than anything else on these platforms. The debilitating effects of this are that we tend to try to live like our electronic friends, and we compare ourselves with them on all conceivable levels. The metrics that we judge ourselves with, are oftentimes biased and are those set by our social media friends (whose existence is doubtful). And, even if they did exist, we are not acquainted with the back story of how they got the success we are admiring.

We go online, and we see a sensational 20-year-old who made millions overnight trading Bitcoin[15]. And that's not all, that same sensational overnight millionaire happens to have a stunning model type of a body. When we see all this, we get all worked up and possibly depressed because, on the other hand, we are forty years old, broke, and in a body we can't even look at in the mirror.

A kid from Africa sees herself not as 'beautiful' because she is busy comparing herself with a model from Brazil. In her view, beauty is long hair, flawless skin, properly curved body. In her comparison, she overlooks factors like natural genes, Photoshop, cosmetics, access to fake hair, nails etc.

My point is that trying to be like our social media-based friends is a terrible idea. The feeling of inadequacy will overwhelm us as what we see online is not what is, and even if it was, there is more to it than what just meets the eye. Don't deprive yourself of life itself by trying to live someone's life. Worse, if that someone is off the internet.

There will only be one you to walk this earth. Show the world what you have. Let the world remember you for being you. Don't let yourself be placed amongst a bunch of copycats and wannabes.

There is a lot of potential and greatness that is waiting to be tapped into, only by you. There is a melodious song that the world hasn't yet heard, a life-changing book not yet written, a piece of art Pablo[16], Leonardo[17] or even Michelangelo[18] died before painting. A speaker of your type hasn't held the mic before. That which has never been Become by anyone is waiting to be Become by you. It could be possible if only you choose to be authentic and not a plagiarizer.

There is nothing wrong in looking up to other people. In fact, it shows that you are smart. Get people who have made it to mentor and inspire you. Subscribe to their blogs. Emulate their success habits. Learn from them – from their strengths, weaknesses and mistakes. Do all this. Yes! But, pay special attention not to end up imprisoning yourself in your own body. Never strive to imitate them to the point of forfeiting your identity.

Learn what you can from people, seek advice and synthesize it however you want it to suit your own purpose. After all, there is nothing new under the sun.

Chapter Summary

The Harsh Reality

We are all going to die

What is the value of your life?

It is determined by:

1. The people you place around yourself

2. The environment you place yourself in

The Japanese way of Living (Ikigai).

1. Do what you love

2. Do what you are good at

3. Do what the world needs

4. Do what you can get paid for

What not to do

Live someone else's life

RURAMAI SITHOLE

CHAPTER SIX

WHAT TO TRUST

"Hold the vision, trust the process."

- Unknown

As a quick recap, the *2nd Law of Becoming* discussed in Chapter 3 calls for us to understand something invaluable. That the size of the goal will determine how much effort and time it will take for us to realize that goal. Big goals demand more effort and time before they can be fully realized. It is that simple, really.

This gives birth to a problem, right? Because many, if not all of us, are pursuing the biggest and craziest goals out there. It's not that there is anything wrong with that, but it's the effort and time we are willing to dedicate towards these dreams that creates the conundrum.

To make it worse, the generation that I am part of is entangled in a catastrophic dilemma. We suffer from the 'I-can't-wait' syndrome! We want answers now, we want solutions yesterday, we want to lose the kilos today, we want the success now and so on. We have, in fact, become an instant-oriented society, and I don't necessarily blame us for this want-it-now attitude.

Our society, with all its advancements, has conditioned us into this state. We have gone from waiting for years for trees and animals to grow, to genetically modifying organisms to mature overnight. Travelling the world has been made very efficient and quite easy. It used to take months to travel across continents, but now it can be done in a day or two. Messaging and communicating is as instant as it can ever get. Through the internet, all questions we have regarding any topic can be answered instantaneously. Microwaves help us cook our food in a very short space of time. We even have 2-minute noodles. Everything nowadays is defined in terms of now.

While these can all be praised as advantageous, the associated adverse effects are subtle and quite detrimental. It has never been as easy to sell any product as it is now. As long as one can explicitly highlight how instantly the results will be reaped – that product will sell. The most downloaded apps are those like the 6-minute abs or the 'Loss 10 kg in 10 days fitness app'. The number of get-rich-quick-schemes being sold and bought out there is baffling. We are all looking for quick fixes, instant results, etc.

Speaking of Get-Rich-Quick-Schemes, once a good friend of mine and I were conned out of a stupendous sum of money. It was back in college, and my friend bumped into this scheme that required us to invest some money for a short time and get a huge payout. When I think about in retrospect, the scheme was just too good to be true. It had something like six hundred percent interest, meaning if we put in a hundred dollar investment, we would make six hundred dollars in a months' time. We would then cash out five hundred bucks and leave another one hundred to be recycled. Easy bucks, right? My friend and I saw this as possibly a chance to make millions and drop out of college immediately. We were gullible enough to invest our hard-earned cash.

I remember my friend and I, budgeting and anticipating the colossal payout that was coming our way. We already knew the fancy clothes, shoes and cars we were going to buy. All was set - except for the money. And you know what they always say, *"Don't ever count your chickens before they're hatched"*. Or, in accounting terminology known as the Prudence concept, *"never anticipate or recognize profits until there is reasonable certainty – in effect."* After depositing a huge figure of money into the investment scheme, the company vanished instantaneously. And that was it. No payout, no car, no fancy shoes, no nothing. We were so deluded and excited by the idea of making millions overnight that we let our guards down. We had fallen into the trap of *wanting-it-now.*

We had forgotten, however, that real, lasting beneficial goals could never be that instant. We had neglected the process.

This is what this chapter is all about - *The Process.* To remind us that the bigger, or the more noteworthy the desired goal is, the less likely it will be realizable or attainable that easily. We cannot demand or expect a cumbersome goal to be satisfied overnight. It is not possible to put our plans and goals into a microwave and wait for the timer to chime after five minutes with all our desired results ready to be enjoyed. It doesn't work that way, unfortunately.

Those of you embarking on the journey to Become must make peace with and acknowledge the process.

Unfortunately, rarely do most of us take into consideration what's required from us to attain our goals when we scribble them down in our diaries or vision boards. And, when we face the actual reality of what is needed from us – it paralyzes us.

It becomes problematic upon squaring up with the fact that the objects of our desires aren't as easily attainable as we would want them to be. The sudden realization of this mandatory process that we need to follow through, sort of kills our passion and zeal. And, this how procrastination sets in. This is when we actually decide it is easier to lie back and not pursue that goal as it appears to be farther from us than we imagined.

See, something called the 'process' is what many of us undervalue when setting out our goals. The process is the journey or the period between when you start pursuing the goal and its final attainment. Few of us are willing to stick to it when it is not instant. The truth of the matter is that goals that genuinely matter aren't as instantaneously realizable as we would want them to be. Becoming is one of these goals that will require us to go through the process.

If We Are To Become then we have to be willing and patient enough to go through the process. This is what we ought to trust on our journey towards Becoming. The process. We must all seek to possess the ability to not be demoralized by the gap between who we are and who we desire to be. It can only be so when we accept this as the truth – that is, it takes a process to get there.

Your Great Wall of China

Of all world wonders, I am forever left awestruck by The Great Wall of China[1]. This wall is undeniably the longest human-made structure on this entire planet and it is located in the northern part of the Republic of China.

What was perhaps a strategic military action centuries ago, has stood the test of time and elements of weather to become a 'world wonder' and the greatest symbol of the Chinese nation. What makes this wall the most amazing and longest feat of human engineering is that it spans over twenty-one thousand kilometers. The wall's peak height is fourteen meters, and its average height ranges between six and seven meters. Just to put this into perspective, this wall's length equals half the equator. This means that two of these walls could span from where you are right now and go around planet earth and right back to where you are (let that sink in for a moment).

This colossal project required more than one million labourers comprising mostly of prisoners, the army, etc. It is claimed that innumerable people died while constructing this wall. They mainly died from exhaustion and hunger and were buried along this wall. This is why some call this wall 'the longest cemetery.'

The first time I was exposed to the construction industry, I was an intern. I worked for a Namibian private company that concentrated on building medium to large structures like shopping malls. Of course, the biggest project I was ever involved in is nothing compared to The Great Wall of China. But, I was appalled by how a forested piece of land could be turned into a magnificent and enormous structure like a mall.

A myriad of activities are enveloped in undertaking construction projects and if I have learned anything from construction, it is, *'to trust the process'.* At the start of every project, if you ascertain the task ahead, you can be left wondering if you'll ever deliver it on time within the prescribed budget and to the required quality standards. But the beauty in construction is, you don't have to do it all at once. There is a process to follow.

It is here that I finally understood the metaphoric concept of taking one step at a time. But in construction, they will not be taking steps but rather laying bricks. So literally, all they will be doing is laying one brick on top of the other and so on. And if the bricks are appropriately laid on top of each other, they will turn into a wall. If you have four of such walls connected together – it turns into a room, and eventually, you will have a building.

And this is how the process works. It is just a matter of laying one brick as perfectly as you can on top of another brick repeatedly until you have a massive structure like the Great Wall.

It is highly unlikely that you are trying to build a 'Great Wall' for your own country. But, carrying such a mindset will catapult you beyond the average in any given field or venture. Understand this: all you need to do is to do the most you can at any given time. If repeatedly done, you will inevitably realize that which you are seeking.

Think of your own wall as that goal you are pursuing and adopt this as the way of achieving it – trusting the process. Tackle it in an itsy-bitsy approach otherwise you'll choke on it if you try swallowing the chunk as a whole. If you lose one kilogram of your body mass per month – in one year, you will have lost twelve. The math is pretty simple – save ten thousand dollars every month. In ten years, you will have one point two million bucks (excluding interest).

I certainly have no idea what wall you are trying to build in your life, but all I know is that to build that wall successfully, you must trust in the process. You must procedurally start laying one brick on top of the other.

At the same time, stand guard and fight the existential urge to focus on the wall itself. It is okay to hold the goal dear in your mind, but you must not get stuck on the actual result.

Hold the vision, trust the process.

Don't go out trying to build a wall. But, go out to lay one brick on top of another brick and continue doing so.

Did you know that The Great Wall of China isn't actually a single wall? The Wall is nothing but pieces of independent walls strung together. If the wall is many pieces of smaller walls, then why won't you build your own 'Great Wall' the same way?

The process does not end at just laying bricks. You ought to join these pieces of separate walls to form a much larger wall. Always remember: four walls built at random are useless. But, if these walls are connected in an orderly fashion, only then can they become useful. This is also true of your wall of Becoming. Make sure all that you are doing, no matter how small, adds something to your wall.

Those who believe in the process

Magic will start to appear as real once you start believing in the process. It is only those who believe that it takes a process to Become who they want to be, who end up Becoming those people. Such people, who believe in the process, are well aware of the task at hand. They know what needs to be done in order to get to where they want to go. And, it is with that in their minds that they do not succumb to the pressures of *wanting-it-now.*

Once you trust the process, you will start sacrificing instant gratification for long-term benefit and not the vice versa. You will develop a farsighted view of your entire life and your goals ahead. A bird's eye view of the journey that lies ahead, so to say. Instead of worrying over how you can erect a skyscraper, you will concentrate on making sure you lay each brick on top of the other as exquisitely as you possibly can. Eventually, that one brick if placed properly on top of the other, will turn into a humungous structure.

However, those who don't believe in the process, have adopted the mantras like; "The end justifies the means." They can't stand the process and inevitably cut corners, cheat, and take the path of least resistance. They are so goal-oriented that they take whatever route that gets them there - even if that route overlooks the process and is unethical. These are the people who will trample over anyone to get there. They will, if given a chance, use other people as stepping stones towards their own fulfilment, and will bulldoze anything or anyone to satisfy their grandiose narcissistic selves. And they always justify their character by claiming its 'doing what it takes'. It is not for me to be judgmental here. However, it is my moral obligation to point out that no matter how far they might go, they cannot be considered as people who have Become. For the purpose of the message in this book, it can never be considered Becoming if it overlooks the process.

As we build our own 'Great Walls,' I suggest that unlike the 'Emperors of China', we must not do it the slavery way. We must not have a million people die building our walls. The walls that we intend to build here are walls we build ourselves. The walls that go through the process. The kind of walls that we place boulder upon boulder as each day passes without losing enthusiasm when we look up ahead of us.

Run your race

Not to sound like I am tooting my own horn, but back in high school, I was a popular kid. One of the many disciplines I was well known for was athletics. Long-distance running to be specific. I competed and won several times in 1500, 2800, and 4800-meter marathon races.

I remember this one time competing in the 4800-meter race (twelve rounds on a 400m track). I ran so fast that I sped across my competitors and passed them twice in that same race. Meaning when I finished the race, my competitors were still short of 800 meters (2 rounds) to finishing (true story; I am not making this up). By the time they finished running, I had already recuperated and was getting ready for my next race.

I learned a lot from this space of marathon running, and one of the lessons I quickly grasped was that even though we were all running the same race, I had to run like was in my own race.

I mean, even though we were all are targeting the 4800-meter mark, the execution didn't necessarily need to be the same. In such races, one would start off jogging while others sprinted, others would save energy and sprint at the end, others would maintain a ¾ pace throughout.

In the race that I resoundingly won, I remember starting off from behind. In fact, I was so far behind that I seemed like a total underdog. But, I had known earlier that the key to winning this race was to run my own race even though we were in the same race. In essence, I was not going to try to run at someone else's pace. If I tried to, chances were that I would have burnt-out and quit. So I remained focused on my execution strategy, knowing when to jog, when to sprint, or use a ¾ pace. And eventually, my competitors who were running in a style that was not like their usual pacing wore themselves down, and they are the ones I ran past twice.

Contrary to popular belief, when you take time to think about it, life is, in actuality, a race. We are all born in this race of life. Believing and trusting in the processes will equip you with a similar perspective towards life. An attitude that might imbue in you a willingness to synonymize life to a marathon open race. A race that all of us have to participate in whether we like it or not.

The truth of the matter is that all of us are racing to get somewhere, get something, be with someone, etc. The tracks of life are the same, but what differs in this race is the 'somewhere,' 'something,' and 'someone.' Unlike the races I competed in, in this race, some are just sprinting for 100 meters, others 200 meters, 400, 1500, 4800, etc. The distances are not fixed nor the same.

People who believe in the process are well acclimated to this immutable truth – that we are in one race, but we have different agendas and targets. Our milestones vary vastly. What becomes imperative is for one to know what his/her targets are and race accordingly.

Imagine trying to keep up with a person sprinting only for 100 meters while you intend to go for 1500 meters. It will probably affect your performance on the remaining 1400 meters. Such is also true in life, even if we are in the same race we must remain attuned to the fact that our agendas are different.

Like the metaphor we were using about building, we are all building, but we aren't building the exact same buildings or walls. There is no need to look around at how or what others are building. Don't try to do it their way. Because for obvious reasons – they might be building a simple wall while you are trying to build a 'Great Wall of China.' You have to lay your bricks as perfectly as you can at your own pace. Don't be rushed or feel pressured by anyone.

Trust in your own process.

You also have to remember that athletes, even in the same race, use different tactics to win. Some train harder, some are naturally talented, the extreme ones will use steroids and stimulating drugs, others will cut lanes, etc. This actually gives you more reason to stick to your process and execution plan because people tend to go about it differently.

We might be all trying to land that promotion or get that job, but some might be well connected or related to whoever has the final say. Some might be willing to taint names to get there. What remains essential is that you lay your bricks. That is what trusting in the process is all about. It is you, remaining true to your execution plan and not losing it even after realizing that your competitors or those you look up to are cutting corners or cheating. When you see someone running way faster than you or doing something you view as close to impossible with so much ease, don't let it falter your motivation. Because we are in the same race but using different execution tactics. Their pace and strength will, and should never be, like ours. Their process and yours are not the same. Trust in yours always.

Understand this: we are no different from popcorn in that:

Popcorn is prepared in the same pot.
Under the same heat,
In the same oil,
But the kernels don't pop at the same time.
Don't compare yourself to others,
Your turn to pop is coming!
–Unknown

When you truly trust in the process, you will stop comparing yourself to anyone else because you'll also understand that we don't pop at the same time. But, eventually, we will all pop. Trusting in the process is like waiting for your time to pop, despite the fact that everyone around you has popped already.

In the Bible, there is a scripture[2] that says in Ecclesiastes 4:

'I have observed something else under the sun. The fastest runner doesn't always win the race, and the strongest warrior doesn't always win the battle. The wise sometimes go hungry, and the skillful are not necessarily wealthy. And those who are educated don't always lead successful lives. It is all decided by chance, by being in the right place at the right time.'

The last part iterates something profound: that *"it is all decided by chance, by being in the right place at the right time."* Another version reads, *"For time and chance happen to all."*

If You Are To Become (Pop), you will have to trust in the process. You will have to understand that time and chance happens to all. You will have to build your wall by laying one brick on top of the other – at your own pace and yours only. You should never allow society to pressure you or impose on you how you should go about it because your time and chance are yet to come, but it surely is coming.

> *A dream delayed is not a dream denied.*

Even if your colleagues or competitors seem to be doing it easily and through other means – you must remain true to your values and soldier on through the process. Once you stick to your process, then you might, just as I did, run past your competitors two times in the same race.

> *Results happen over time, not overnight*
> *Work Hard, Stay Consistent, and*
> *Be Patient.*
> *–Unknown*

Chapter Summary

What to trust

How to build your Great Wall.

DO it procedurally.

Concentrate on laying one single brick on top of another brick.

Trusting the process

Those who believe in the process;

–choose long term benefit over instant gratification.

Running your own race

The only person you should be competing against, is your yesterday–self.

CHAPTER SEVEN

EMBRACING TO BECOME

"Let me embrace thee, sour adversity, for wise men say it is the wisest course."

- Henry VI Part III, William Shakespeare

In his book 'The 7 Habits of Highly Effective People', Stephen R. Covey[1] tells us that there is a *sphere of concern* and *a sphere of influence.* The former constitutes all that we worry about; our health, relationships, politics, weather, emigration laws, etc. The latter, however, is made up of all that we have direct influence or control over; our health status, what we wear, the job we take on, who we date, and so on.

Covey defines reactive people as those who concentrate their forces on issues in the sphere of concern, where, unfortunately, the related outcomes are beyond their control. He goes on to point out that *proactive individuals* are those who expend their energy and time only to what is in their sphere of influence, - where they call all the shots.

What the weather will be like tomorrow, whether nations decide to embark on a world-war-three venture or whether we wake up dead, is, unfortunately, far from our control. So, here is my question: why on earth do we get all worked up fretting over issues that are beyond our control? And worse still, when we know that nothing will change, no matter how much we worry over them?

True and lasting self-empowerment emanates from the realization that we might be concerned about a lot of stuff, but there is only a portion over what we can influence. Key to Becoming is focusing on those issues that we can direct and ignoring what we just can't control.

Simply put, you can only be a master of your fate or a captain of your soul over issues in your area of influence.

What to Avoid

John B. Watson[2] is a man who left his mark in the annals of psychology. His famous, or rather infamous, experiment[3] was one that he and Rosalie Rayner[4] performed to prove that fear was a response that could be attained through classical conditioning[5].

In the experiment, they wanted to prove that fear was not real – that it was just a learned response acquired through some form of conditioning. To achieve this they took an infant baby boy called Albert and carried out a series of emotional and experimental tests. Watson and Rayner exposed Albert to furry animals (including a white rat) and other items he had never encountered before like fury masks, burning newspapers, dogs etc. For someone who was seeing all this for the first time, Albert did not show any sign of fear, but rather, due to curiosity, he reached out to touch these items.

Then, they set the conditioning into play by hanging a steel bar close to "Little Albert" and struck it with a hammer each time he tried to touch the white rat. They repeatedly carried out this process, producing a startling sound whenever the boy tried to touch the rat. The resultant effects were that presenting a white rat to Albert would scare the living hell out of him, leading him to cry. In fact, when other furry items were placed near him, he would crawl away for his dear life.

What had happened to this little fellow? He had at first shown an interest towards these items, but now anything furry seemed to upset his mood. Little Albert had undergone classical conditioning, and for him – it involved associating the loud, unbearable, and ear-piercing noise with anything furry.

The repeated pairing of the white rat and the loud noise led to Albert fearing white rats or anything furry for that matter.

Below is an illustration of Little Albert's classical conditioning.

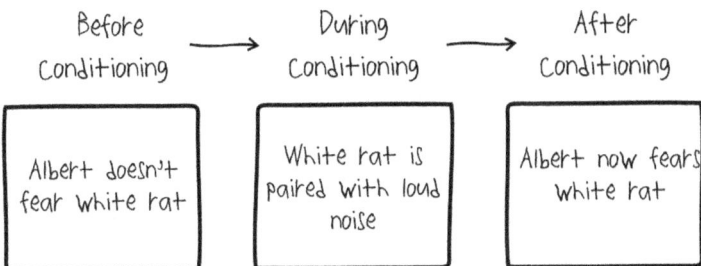

Before Conditioning		During Conditioning		After Conditioning
Albert doesn't fear white rat	→	White rat is paired with loud noise	→	Albert now fears white rat

If you did not already know this, classical conditioning is one of the three ways we learn anything in this world. And we are all very much like Little Albert. Only that we aren't dealing with a bunch of furry items and startling metallic sounds. Yet, our situation is of the same nature and let me tell you why.

What to Embrace

See, there is something that most of us, if not all, have come to dread, and we do all we can do every single day to avoid crossing paths with it. We design and shape our lives to make sure we don't experience that 'something.' Because, well, we have misinterpreted what it really is. Going through this 'something' is considered shameful.

It is appalling to note that this creature, that we all strive to avoid is, in actuality, the *Prince Charming* underneath the frog. It has been grossly misunderstood and falsely accused. This unwanted and must-avoid-at-all-cost-creature is the secret ingredient to us ever Becoming. It is the icing for our perfectly baked cake called life. Those who have chosen and taken delight in embracing it have conquered life, ruled men, and amassed wealth. Its existence has made every success story enticing and inspiring.

What is this thing?

You might have already guessed it. I am talking about **personal adversity!**

Since we blame everything on society, allow me to point my finger at it as well. Society has classically conditioned us into ill-defining what adversity really is. We have allowed negative experiences to be blown out of proportion and we keep placing too much value on them. Consequently, we have tended to inflate the significance that adversity has in our lives. We do what we can to the best of our capabilities not go through adversarial moments because of whatever reasons we hold in our belief system. One can quickly be dubbed as incompetent or a failure for going through some negative situations or rough patches in life. We have paired adversity with failure, just like how 'Little Albert' paired the loud noise with the white rat.

Stay with me on this one. What makes us no different from 'Little Albert' is the fact that before our conditioning, we were just as curious as him. We reached out to anything, and we tried everything, not worrying about the consequences or what people around us would think. At one point, we didn't care how many times we fell while trying to walk. We fell countless times and probably hurt ourselves before finally learning how to walk. That was a 'Becomers attitude' in play. Somewhere along the journey of life, we met our own 'Watson & Rayners', who told us that our attitude was a dangerous way of living. They told us it was not okay to try something that we had no guarantee of succeeding at. For some, this conditioning was through a flawed educational system that graded and labelled them as smart only to a certain level. This placed glass ceilings over their heads.

For some, it was an unhealthy upbringing. Sticking to a certain area that they could really excel at was applauded – while trying to step into new territories and with the possibility of failing at them was shunned. I believe this is what led them to seek and resolve to stay in their comfort zones and never step outside of them.

Why? Because let's face it, negative situations and experiences are undesirable and painful, and obviously, no sane parent or guardian would want us to seek them. It is even worse, considering that we have been conditioned to pair such negative situations with failure. We try by all means to avoid anything that might have us looked at as failures. By trying not to go through it, we suffer the consequences of staying where we are safe and sound (the comfort zone). And when adversity finally hits, which is inevitable in this journey called life, we will not be able to deal with it because we lack the proper mindset and because we already have this disproportionate view of adversity. Its effects become more devastative than they should be.

Here is my suggestion. How about we embrace the inevitable and redefine it to work to our advantage? In my view, embracing is far much better than total avoidance because, at the end of the day, there is no way of totally avoiding it. Adversity is beyond our control, and for that reason, as the proactive people who are on the road to Becoming, we should not even waste a second of our lives worrying or crying over it. Instead, I propose we embrace personal adversity as it comes.

Since we don't get to choose what happens to us, how about we decide what it should mean to us, and how to respond to it? *If We Are To Become*, the best response towards adversity is to embrace it.

Have you ever realized what inspires us most in success stories? It's the existence of a negative story; how one conquered an adverse circumstance. The triumph over obstacles is what speaks volumes to us. So hey, why not find solace in the fact that unfavourable events occur to colour your success story. You know what they all say, *"The harder the battle, the sweeter the victory."*

However, personal adversity is a broad subject and encapsulates most commonly mistakes, rejections, betrayals, losses, and criticisms, amongst other things.

I want us to dissect these five in particular and see how we often misinterpret them. How we can adopt them as propellants towards success instead of allowing them to deter us from Becoming the best of who we can be.

Mistakes

Has it ever occurred to you that all we see in this world, all the inventions that shape the world we live in today, resulted from 'Trial and Error[6]'? Seriously think about it. Someone had to envision an item that no one at that time had ever seen. Since it was being created for the first time, it had to be achieved through Trial and Error. It was just a matter of trying out anything and everything in the hope that it would somehow work. Out of those numerous Trials and Errors came out what we see today. Someone had to try different combinations of chemicals in order to create ink. Thanks to that person, I am able to write to you, and you are able to read it. All because of Trial and Error.

Trial and Error has taken us from inhabiting caves and wearing animal skins; from walking barefooted across plains and hunting with primitive rock weapons, to what we see today - being able to be doing what you are currently doing now; reading. To not only sending messages through the air but to travelling through the air as well.

The people who have managed to shape civilization and the world as it is, are the people who have experimented with life.

It's the people who have intentionally sought out mistakes that have brought us this far. It is not far-fetched then, to suggest that the world revolves around mistakes. When you take time to think about it, Trial and Error are mistakes intentionally made until a desired outcome is attained.

Mistakes stacked on top of other mistakes have been perfected and have propelled the human species. Mistakes have redirected our civilization on the ascent we are currently on. The willingness to try, fail, learn, and try again, fail, and continue learning, has advanced us to where we are right now.

I find it appalling however, that we have managed to embrace the Trial and Error mindset everywhere else except in our own lives. Whenever we make mistakes, we rarely see them as failed trials that need perfection.

As humans, we should, by now, have come to terms with the fact that we are far from perfect. And, for that reason, we are all guilty of making mistakes. Some make mistakes more frequently than others. Others make mistakes on trivial matters, others on life-and-death situations. Some appear to make mistakes more than anything else, while others seem never to make mistakes at all (but they do). Some mistakes have negative effects, while some have positive effects.

Some of the most famous inventions were a result of mistakes. The Penicillin antibiotic, for example, was discovered unintentionally by Fleming. My point is, we all make mistakes. We all do and we will continue making them.

> *Not only are mistakes common, but
> they are also very necessary.*

No one exhibited as much of an understanding that mistakes were indeed necessary, as Alva. Alva was born in 1847, in Milan, Ohio. The only formal education Alva had lasted for just three months at a public school. Luckily his mother was a teacher who homeschooled him until he was proficient in reading and writing. However, he developed a passion for experimenting with chemicals – just to verify the validity of information in textbooks. It soon morphed into a hobby, and he turned the cellar into his little private laboratory.

To fund this amateur-like inexpensive venture, he needed income. At age eleven, Alva was compelled to start selling vegetables at a port. By age twelve, he was working as a newspaper boy servicing two stations a hundred kilometers apart. Through some persuasion, he later managed to convert the baggage car of a train into his printing press and a lab concomitantly. Unfortunately, it was in this train car that an accident occurred and left him deaf in 1862 – age fifteen. After getting kicked off this train – Alva settled for a regular job as a telegraphist. No one could have ever imagined that this boy was going to be one of the greatest inventors to have walked this earth.

Amongst his other inventions, Alva was celebrated for discovering the incandescent light bulb. Oh yeah! – I am talking about the celebrated Thomas Alva Edison[7].

I am convinced that the backstory of Thomas' upbringing had so much influence on his later career achievements. What's never talked about pertaining to this light bulb project, is that this project had been dubbed as "practically beyond attainment[8]." In fact, this had been a hot topic among electricians, leading experts, *physicists, and geniuses before Mr Edison worked on it. For more than a quarter-century, the science gurus had tried to come up with a working bulb and failed dismally. This explains why the bulb project had been termed as "practically beyond attainment". When he started his experiments in 1877, Thomas was well aware of these failed efforts.*

Fast-forward to October 1879, the initial breakthrough was recorded as a bulb using a carbonized cotton thread as a filament. This bulb could stay on and last up to forty-five hours before the filament's disintegration. The rest is history.

Unless you are reading this book from Utopia[9], then mistakes are going to be part of your journey. A wise philosopher once said, *'there are no mistakes in life, only lessons.'* This philosopher was not suggesting that this is a mistake-free world, but rather that if interpreted and embraced properly, mistakes can serve as valuable lessons.

Thomas interpreted mistakes through the 'Trial & Error' lenses, and it saw him through the attainment of his incredible inventions. He persevered, despite knowing that what he sought to achieve had been tried by people with more skills, capital, etc. For him to find a suitable filament, it is said, he literally carbonized anything and everything he could get his hands on. He went on to try different species of grass to tissue paper, bamboo, twine, coconut hair, fish-lines, cotton, you name it. The claim is that he had carbonized and made into lamps all these random materials. For the two years he spent working on the bulb, he had tested a staggering sum of over six thousand different materials (tell me that's not something).

When asked how he felt and what kept him going despite failing to light up the bulb after thousands of attempts, he responded, *"I didn't fail a thousand of times, I only found a thousand ways that did not work."*

Most of us move through life, avoiding the inevitable occurrence of mistakes because of the misconception we have towards them. What we tend to forget, however, is that mistakes are not permanent. That they are just bruises and not tattoos. Our mistakes do not define us. Rather, they play a part in shaping us - if we allow them to. We all make them, and those who receive praise have probably failed more than the rest of us.

> *Both the "successful" and the "loser" fail at something, but one fails and learns while the other fails to learn.*
> *– Magic of Thinking Big[10]*

Embracing mistakes:

1. Take full responsibility.
   Don't give in to the temptation to pass the blame. Take full ownership of your mistakes because they are yours.
2. Understand and appreciate that we all make mistakes.
   No one is immune from making mistakes. Even the sharpest and most brilliant minds make errors. Who are you to think that you can't or shouldn't make mistakes?
3. Find a thing or two to learn from each mistake.
   There is always something to learn from every mistake. In fact, that's where the growth is. Only after asking yourself

what you did wrong can you guarantee that you won't make that same mistake in the future.

4. Avoid making the same mistake twice.

That is the whole point; to learn and grow from mistakes. After learning from them, we should strive not to make those same mistake again.

5. Embrace 'Trial and Error' as a way to flourish.

No one has lived your life before, and you are living your life the first time. You need to approach it with a 'Trial and Error' mindset. Just throw everything and anything to the wall and see what sticks.

Rejections

Here is something rather painful. Somewhere along this journey called life, you and I and everyone else you know will face rejection a couple of times. The immutable truth is that rejections are inevitable — and we have zero influence towards them occurring to us.

You will get rejected by your lover, your job application will be declined, and your business proposal turned down. The bank loan application will be brushed aside, your projects dismissed, your input will be looked down upon in meetings. There are certain events or places you will be denied entry into. The list of possible rejections is just but endless. Rejections come and go. But, only those who understand this truth can transcend above the norm.

JK Rowling[11]'s rise to stardom represents what it truly means to embrace rejections at its highest form. Just as she started writing the first chapters of her book at age twenty-five, she lost her mother, which left her shattered and in despair. After moving to Spain, she got married, had a miscarriage, before later giving birth to her daughter. Her marriage fell apart after thirteen months.

Now, as a single mother, she again moved to Britain. She was unemployed and had to survive on state benefits, while pursuing her writing dream. After manually typing her '90000-word' manuscript, she sent it to various publishers. The book she had spent years writing, the only lifeline she was desperately clinging onto, was rejected. The book was not just rejected by one publisher; but, it was turned down by twelve publishers. Yes! Twelve publishers thought that her book was not good enough to sell. This rejection spiraled her into a deep depression.

She confesses that it pushed her even to consider suicide as an escape plan. She had totally lost confidence in her dream – her book. As luck would have it, one small publisher decided to give the book a try. Not because they thought it was a great book – but because the CEO's daughter had fallen in love with the manuscript. Thanks to that CEO's daughter – otherwise, JK Rowling would not have become the JK Rowling we know today.

JK Rowling's book series has broken multiple records, and an estimate of over 450 million copies have been sold worldwide. Not only have her books shaken the book industry, but they have also claimed their space in the movie industry. In 2001, Forbes listed JK Rowling as a billionaire and she remains one of the top-earning authors to this date.

Who would have thought that an unemployed, divorced single mother would be as influential as she is today? In fact, who would have imagined that a book rejected by more than twelve publishers had a chance of selling even a hundred copies? More importantly, after being rejected that many times, why did she even bother pursuing that career?

Some of us never ask a single thing from the universe. We never apply for any opportunity, never ask for help, never look for capital to fund our ideas, never ask for that promotion, never ask that lady out on a date.

Why?

Because we fear getting rejected. We don't want to hear the phrase, NO! We resolve to not ask for anything because we have associated rejection with the idea that it would mean that, us or our work is not good enough. Nothing could be farther from the truth because, as we have learned, JK Rowling's book was good enough. Yet it was rejected twelve times.

We should never hesitate to ask for what we desire because we fear rejection. And, when we do get rejected, we should never let that put us down.

The problem with us not asking from the world what we desire, is that not everyone is telepathic (I doubt anyone is anyway). No one can read minds. No one will ever know what you want, unless you ask for it.

There is an African proverb that says:

> *A child who does not cry will die unnoticed on its mother's back.*

Let us imagine: you are languishing in this dark corner of misery. You know precisely what you want - what could drag you out of that dark place you are in. You know the person who has that something in abundance. All you have to do is ask, but for some reason, you dread hearing that person say NO! So what do you do? You resort to getting used to that uncomfortable pity-corner of yours while wishing and hoping somebody could save you. I want to ask you this: what do you lose by just asking? I mean, if that person says NO, what difference does it make? You are already in that situation, and rejection will not put you in a worsened situation than you are already in. You are already in it, so what is the big fuss? After all, *it's the squeaky wheel that will always get the grease.*

You might say;

"Oh wait, but my Harvard application was rejected." So what? You were not at Harvard anyway, were you?

"I didn't get that promotion." Sorry about that, but you weren't a manager all this time, remember?

"She refused to go on date with me." She wasn't your date before you asked.

It is all a matter of perspective. It is how we perceive these rejections that will determine if we ask for it or not in the future. And, it is also a matter of how much we ask for it that determines our chance of getting it. If there is the slightest chance of a YES, no matter how small it is, then you lose nothing by asking. ASK. ASK. And ASK!!!

If you get rejected at anything, which will happen one way or the other, all you can do is reflect on that rejection and you ASK AGAIN!

If We Are To Become, we have to be willing to get some No's before getting a Yes. What's critical is that we keep soldiering on no matter how many No-Entry-Sign-Posts we meet along the way. Salespeople have understood this very well – it's all a game of numbers. If your conversion rate is four percent - meaning out of every hundred people you approach, only four buy your product – that means, to make forty sales, you have to contact a thousand prospective buyers. Nine hundred sixty will decline, but forty will buy-in. That is what embracing rejections means - it's the ability and willingness to receive nine hundred and sixty no's while remaining focused on acquiring only forty yes's. But truth be told, few of us are willing to endure that much rejection.

Most of us quit upon meeting the first sign of rejection. JK Rowling didn't give up despite being rejected that much. She held her dream firmly until it became a reality. The book she had started writing when she was twenty-five was published when she was thirty-two and went on to change her entire life.

This is what I want for you: to have Rowling's tenacity and attitude. To persevere in the face of rejection. To never believe that the only way to protect yourself is to not ask for it. I want you to understand that by not asking you stand no chance of getting it. I want you to keep asking, no matter how many times you get rejected.

You must keep believing, even when it seems that no one believes in you. Remaining adamant in the face of rejection is a prerequisite for every dreamer.

Let me share with you how you can embrace your rejections:
1. Remind yourself of who/where you were before that rejection happened.Most of the time, we get phased over

rejections and we somehow forget that nothing has changed from who/where we were before that rejection happened. If she said no to your proposal; does it change anything? Considering that you were single before she said no and you are still single after she said no.

2. Don't forget your worth.

   You should never let rejections define you or lower your self-esteem. If your business pitch is turned down, it doesn't mean you suck as a human being. Never inflate the significance that a rejection has in your life.

3. Understand that it is not final.

   One man's meat is another man's poison.

   If you believe that you or your idea is not poison, continue looking for the man who sees it as meat.

4. Be open-minded and don't take it personally.

   Consider that maybe, you, your idea or your plan is not as good as you think it is.

   Receiving and accepting a rejection with an open mind is acknowledging that there could be some shortcomings to your plans.

5. Re-evaluate and flourish.

   Think it through and go on to use that rejection as a stepping stone towards your next business pitch, your future relationship, etc.

Losses

He was nicknamed 'The American Miler,' while some referred to him as the 'Kansas Ironman.' If you had told him that he was going to run again when he was seven years old, I bet he would have cursed you with every word in the dictionary. When he was only seven, he and his brother Floyd were involved in a classroom explosion. Unfortunately, Floyd passed on during this incident. On the other hand, Glenn (the ironman) was left in such a state that he probably wished he had died with his brother. His lower body was burnt to the extent that amputation seemed to be the more straightforward solution. His physicians were convinced that he would never walk again, that is, if he survived (which they highly doubted). To a regular person, this is the real definition of losing. Most would accept this, simply lie down, never to stand again. But, to Glenn Cunningham[12], this was not enough to keep him down.

After spending months in a hospital being closely monitored, he would later give his all towards walking again. They say, "A journey of a thousand miles begins with a single step", and surely for Glen, that single step led to a much more extraordinary journey. Not a walking journey, but a running one.

Years after being told he would never walk again, he would go on to break multiple records. He set six records for the one-mile race, a record for the 1500 mile race, amongst others. *"The story of determination"* as it has been dubbed epitomizes what it means to embrace losses as they happen. Despite losing his brother, his ability to walk and almost losing his life, Glen did not stop hoping. These events were not enough to beat him down permanently. In fact, they ignited him to aspire to do the somewhat impossible – and he surely did. By embracing his loss, Glen was able to become much more than he was before he faced his predicament. Relatively speaking, he had every reason to gripe at life and play the victim (because he was). Still, he chose not to, and that very attitude elevated him to be 'The Kansas Ironman.'

I have come to believe that losing is, without a doubt, the way of life. Has it ever occurred to you that from the moment we are born, we start losing? We start losing our time here on earth. We lose the direct attachment we have to our mothers. As we grow older, we lose our infancy benefits and privileges, and we lose our fair skins and hair. Later we lose our seeing, hearing, walking, and even talking abilities. By this time, we would have lost countless people, jobs, assets, etc. Eventually we'll end up losing our lives and that's just the way it is.

Many of us go through life making a big deal of every loss incurred when, in actual fact, we should make peace with the fact that losing is inevitable. Losing is the reason for being. It is necessary and inescapable.

Losing, to humans is what sloughing is to snakes. Periodically as snakes grow in size, their skins expand, and slough off. Which means, a snake has to lose its old skin to have a newer, shiny one. The same applies to the human species; losing has brought us to where we are today. How else would we know the joys of being on a mountain top unless we have once been in a valley? We value light because we have once been in the dark. It is because we have experienced certain circumstances in life that we view the world through these lenses. Losing that person was necessary so we could appreciate life more. Your boyfriend or girlfriend dumping you paved the way for someone who loved you the same way you loved them. If you hadn't lost that life-sucking-job, you would not have lived every single day doing what you love.

> *If you feel like you're losing something/everything, remember that trees lose their leaves every year And, they still stand tall and wait. They wait for better days to come.*

However, what remains critical is the narrative we choose to tell ourselves once we lose. We don't determine what happens to us, but we can choose what it means to us. This explains why two people losing on the same front can be affected by it in two totally different ways.

Embracing Losses:

1. Understand that everybody loses.

   To be genuinely free, we need to acknowledge this as a fact. At one point, we are going to have to deal with losses in life. It is not possible to go through life without losing something or someone. That's just the way it is.

2. Choose what losing means to you.

   Since we can't choose what happens to us, why not choose what to make of it. Because at the end of the day, it is what we choose to tell ourselves in the face of losses, that determines if we make it out or not. We should tell ourselves, therefore, whatever narrative that serves us to go forward.

3. Imagine the possible 'worst-case' scenario that could have happened.

The fact of the matter is, no matter what you have lost, it is nothing compared to the worst possible scenario. In every loss, you should take comfort in knowing that you are not facing the worst possible loss. It could have been more, but luckily it is not, and that's something to be grateful for.

4. Feel the pain, but don't get stuck on it.

   I am not advising you to avoid entertaining negative emotions. Embracing losses is not about feeling good when your entire world has just crushed.

   It is okay to be sad or feel pained- don't try to avoid it. Feel it, but don't live in that pain forever.

5. Get ready for future losses.

   Losing is unavoidable, and the more prepared you are for future losses, the better. I am not preaching pessimism – I am just giving it to you as it is.

Criticisms

Am I the only one who is bummed by people who shrink in the face of criticism? People who let other people beat them down by what they think about their work and their lives.

Some people expect life to be smooth and easygoing, - like a sunny stroll in the park. But that world doesn't exist anymore, that is if it ever existed anyway. We find ourselves living in a world full of critics. Everybody and anybody is somehow an 'expert' at everything. Everyone feels entitled to air out what they think about other people, their business, and their work. On social media, you find a 'nobody' arguing and criticizing someone well versed in the subject being talked about. Everything nowadays is reviewed, from food to art, music, user experience, and so on. We are in the age of the 'critics'. One should never, even for a second, think that he/she is immune to criticism because critics are lurking everywhere. The world is suffocating with critics and naysayers, and we should never let them get to us.

Some people believe that if they do great things, they will not face any opposition, let alone criticism. Nothing could be farther from the truth because criticism is actually worse for someone trying to do something big. Once you pursue greatness, you will have isolated and spotlighted yourself. By placing yourself in the arena of Becomers, you will attract more critics than you ever have before.

The fact is, only when you're doing something worthwhile will you face opposition. Because *'action and reaction are always equal and opposite.'* So, in essence, if no one is opposing you, then you aren't doing anything noticeable or worth opposing. Those who are doing big things are dealing with a lot of opposition.

Because:

> *The tree that bears fruit will be stoned.*
> *– Turkish Proverb*

Take heed of the words from the 26th President of the United States of America, Theodore Roosevelt[13], in his famous *"The Man in the Arena"* speech[14]:

> *"It is not the critic who counts; not the man who points out how the strong man stumbles, or where the doer of deeds could have done them better. The credit belongs to the man who is actually in the arena, whose face is marred by dust and sweat and blood; who strives valiantly; who errs, who comes short again and again,*

because there is no effort without error and shortcoming; but who does actually strive to do the deeds; who knows great enthusiasms, the great devotions; who spends himself in a worthy cause; who at best knows, in the end, the triumph of high achievement, and who at the worst, if he fails, at least fails while daring greatly, so that his place shall never be with those cold and timid souls who neither know victory nor defeat."

You definitely won't be able to make everyone as pleased as you would want them to be. However, if you are convinced that whatever you are doing is for the greater good, and you are not harming or stepping on anyone, then march forward and view those critics as your fans who just have a hard time showing it.

The ripest mango will have the most stones thrown at it.

However, if you insist that you really don't want to be criticized then you have to say nothing, do nothing, and be nothing. And, I doubt that is what you want. That is not what I want for you either. You cannot Become if you literally say, do, or be nothing. Understand this: as you become, so will you be criticized and opposed.

But wait, there is more.

Still, on the issue of criticism, not every criticism is fueled by hate. Not everyone who is criticizing you wishes you harm. I have found that most times, due to emotions invested in what we are pursuing – we lack objectivity. We rarely manage to honestly and objectively assess our capabilities in that regard. In fact, most of the time, we see ourselves better than we actually are in reality (see Chapter 2).

Part of embracing criticism is managing our egos not to go ahead of us. To not be misled by our over-inflated egotistic selves. Honest and positive criticism is something we should all yearn of receiving. Sometimes it takes someone other than ourselves to evaluate our work and efforts.

I have learned this through my journey as a speaker and member of the Toastmasters International. Each time I deliver a speech, I receive feedback afterwards. The input is based on what I would have done well and what I could have done differently to excel. It is from these feedbacks that I have grown and become a better speaker altogether.

In this regard, life is similar to speaking; you don't really know if your speech was impactful or not. In your head, you might be killing it, but it takes someone other than you to confirm that you are actually killing it. And, if you are not killing it, you can be advised on how you can do so next time.

Without people advising and critiquing us on what we are not seeing, we could lose it all. We might not like being criticized, but sometimes we definitely need it to step into our next level.

However, it's critical that you:

1. Monitor where the criticism is coming from.

Usually, it's best that we listen to people who have been to where we want to be. Every Jack and Jill has something to say about anything and everything. Filter the voices you pay attention to.

2. Never take it personal.

Most of the time, it is not about you as a person. Detach all emotions and seek to learn a thing or two about your work and how others perceive it.

3. Always find the positive takeaway from every criticism.
    Approach every form of criticism with a perspective that it's being given in good faith. Only disregard it after comprehensively listening to it first.

4. Don't be defensive.
    Listen to understand, and do not be quick to go on the defensive-mode. Don't try to justify or make excuses – Listen first!

5. Say thank you.
    It would be best if you appreciated those who have taken their time to give you honest feedback. Imagine if they saw what you were doing incorrectly and decided not to tell you.

Do not let criticism put you down in any way. There is always something to gain from every criticism. We first need to approach it with an open mind and with the hope that we can grow from it. However, if its criticism not given in good faith, we can choose to disregard it. After all, not everyone wishes us well.

Good or bad criticism will be thrown at you from all angles, and In any case, it's imperative to keep our ego in check.

Betrayals

What happens when the people who are supposed to look out for you are the ones who betray you? Or the people you trust are the ones that stab you? I presume it is not a hard scenario to imagine because chances are you have probably been let down once or twice, and you surely know how heart-piercing it is.

The common saying these days is, "people are fake!"

It's like out of nowhere people suddenly thrive on backstabbing. It's the new norm, I suppose.

Listen to what Trent Shelton[16] has to say on this subject, *"Life has taught me that you can't control someone's loyalty. No matter how good you are to them, doesn't mean they'll treat you the same. No matter how much they mean to you, doesn't mean they'll value you the same. Sometimes the people you love the most, turn out to be the people you can trust the least"*.

When I read those words, I felt them. They hit me on the spot. I jumped up and down as I chowed on those profound words. Is there anyone who could have packaged it more magnificently than this?

People you know will screw you countless times for no reason and sometimes for a reason (but it's still screwing over). In the Bible; the story of Joseph[17] depicts total betrayal on the highest level.

Joseph was the last born in a family of twelve brothers, and he was also a dreamer. Like literally, he could dream and interpret dreams linking them to some future events. He, of course, being the last born, was the most favoured child in the family. Compounded by the fact that he was talented, his brothers started to resent him and became jealous of him.

It is written in the book of Genesis[18] that Joseph visited his brothers at the pastures and they turned on him, tied him up and imprisoned him in a well. The brothers, to cover up their tracks, took Joseph's clothes, spilt animal blood all over them, and claimed that a wild beast had devoured him. They later traded Joseph for coins to some foreign traders who took him to Egypt as a slave.

As a reminder, here's what Trent Shelton said, *"no matter how much they mean to you, it doesn't mean they will value you the same."*

And in Joseph's case, his betrayal didn't come from strangers; it came from the people who were supposed to protect him the most – his family.

Joseph's life as a slave had a lot of ups and downs. He was once framed by his master's wife for attempted rape and was jailed for that crime. From being a prisoner, he went on to interpret Pharaoh's dream and earned himself a highly coveted post in Egypt. Not only did that interpretation save Egypt from calamitous drought, but it also managed to save Joseph's family when they came in need of food supplies. Joseph's story has a 'Happily Ever After' type of an ending.

While you might not have Joseph's heart to forgive your betrayers – it remains your task to embrace betrayals with the right mindset. Knowing that anyone and everyone can betray you despite your relationship with them, can be a freeing experience. Accepting that betrayals are not in your area of influence should allow you not to be taken aback or view them as major obstacles in your life.

This shouldn't scare or prevent us from ever committing to anything or anyone. It is prudent for you as an aspiring Becomer to eliminate any room to entertain the fear of being betrayed. If you eliminate this fear of betrayal, only then could you be able to find someone to partner with on a business venture. Who knows?

Maybe you could then find yourself in a meaningful and healthy relationship and commit without any doubt or stress of what tomorrow holds. In any case, all you can do is to play your part and let the rest figure itself out.

To embrace Betrayals, we need to:

1. Avoid the temptation to retaliate.

   This is the hardest thing to do. We must fight the incessant urge to get back at our betrayers. You must choose to be the better person. Don't be like them – you are better than them.

2. Detach yourself from the situation.

   Take some time-out, mate. It helps fight the urge to retaliate. If you don't step out of the situation, you will probably lash out and act impulsively and regrettably.

3. Reflect and Grow.

   A step further than detaching from the situation is that we reflect on the betrayal and grow from it. Sometimes through reflection, you will see a part you played or the warning signs you chose to ignore before you received this blow.

4. Have a chat with the betrayer (if possible).

   If you can chat with your betrayer, it might give you closure if you desperately need it. However, don't count too much on getting anything out of this.

5. Forgive.

   Forgive! Forgive! Forgive! Nothing more, nothing less, just forgive.

Learning to Embrace

It has become apparent that adversity occurs with or without your consent. You are bound to make mistakes, lose, be rejected, criticized, and even betrayed. It remains somewhat inevitable, and I want to urge you to never allow any form of adversity to:

1. Belittle your past, by making you angry or sad,
2. Mar your present by making you uneasy or
3. Diminish your future by pumping anxiety into your vulnerable self.

Both fretting over past adversities and fearfully living while imagining a future infested by adversity does not serve you in any way. It only derails you.

Let's work on the present. Let's live today only. Living today empowers us beyond your wildest imagination. It equips us with the power to embrace and soak in the adversity.

Avoid monumentalizing adversities

Whatever happened - happened, what's going to happen, will happen, and when it does let us see it as the healable bruise it is, and not as a permanent tattoo.

To think that one can avoid making mistakes, losing, getting rejected, betrayed, or criticized, is like believing that tomorrow the sun will not come up. It's just not possible, and the sooner we make peace with that, the better.

Let's learn from these negative circumstances no matter how undesirable they are – remember a champion can only be called champion after going through multiple adversaries. Not necessarily overcoming them but just going through them.

But that is not enough, just going through negative situations and circumstances is not enough for us to Become. If We Are To Become, we will not only have to GO through adversity – we will also have to GROW through it.

Don't just GO through adversity
GROW through it.

There is a saying that goes *'If you ask GOD for growth, then be willing to be rained upon.'* Just like how we grow muscles in the gym; we have to continuously tear and heal through vigorous exercises. Personal adversity is necessary, just like how pain is necessary to grow muscle. What makes some individuals a cut above the rest in the gym and everywhere else in life, is their ability to withstand pain. They acknowledge that it is part of the growth process and intentionally go through the tearing and healing, knowing that, that's where the growth lies.

To be able to embrace negative situations and to persist in difficult and undesirable times is not only important, but it is necessary. You have to remember that even losers can keep going when they are winning. To join the league of titans like Thomas Edison, JK. Rowling, Joseph, Glenn Cunningham, etc. you have to embrace all forms of adversity life throws your way. The character of champions is forged through adversity.

When all seems lost.
When all seem to be fighting you.
When the road becomes bumpier than before.
The weather becomes harsher.
The destination seems farther and unreachable.
When giving up looks like the only option.
When this happens;
Remind yourself why you started

Chapter Summary

Embracing to Become

We must avoid:

(The Little Albert Effect)

Mistaking adversity for failure

We should embrace:

Personal Adversity

We should grow through:

- *Mistakes*
- *Rejections*
- *Losses*
- *Criticisms*
- *Betrayals*

To grow we must:

Avoid monumentalizing adversity

CHAPTER EIGHT

BECOMING TO LEAD

*Attend To Your Own Personal Development. "Everyone thinks of
changing the world, but no one thinks of changing himself."*
– Leo Tolstoy.

Once you decide to pursue Becoming, you have, in other words, chosen to become a leader. One's level of Becoming can be best illustrated by how much that person can lead in the real world. Just so I make sure we are all on the same page, perhaps let's interrogate what a leader is.

Of course, leadership is too broad a subject to be enveloped in just a single definition. For us, however, a leader will be best described as any person seeking positive change in any environment. If you have ever said something like, *'I want to change the world,' 'I want to make the world a better place,' 'I want to be remembered for the good I brought into this world,'* etc., all of that is synonymous to saying *'I want to be a leader'*. Most, if not all of us who set out to 'change the world' fail dismally because of the gross misconception that we have with regards to leadership.

I am going to show you how this is so in a moment.

By now, I am confident that you desire to Become, and this should not come as a shocker that you are inevitably going to be a leader. You will not necessarily need a fancy-leadership title for you to be "the leader." Still, by virtue of who you would have Become on the inside, you will have a voice even when your mouth is shut.

Only after you have Become will you find yourself in William[1] Kamkwamba's shoes (The Boy Who Harnessed the Wind) mentioned in Chapter 1. People will feel the urge to want to listen to you, copy you, and be around you. They will believe and buy into whatever you have to say. And, by that, my friend, you will be an ordained leader. But, it is not a direct route from A to B – there's a multi-stage process that is mandatory to follow if we ever want to be leaders. This is where the aforementioned 'gross misunderstanding' comes into effect—thinking that you can simply just go out and change the world. Nothing could be farther from the truth. Going from today (who and where you are) to tomorrow (changing the world) is not as easy and direct as it sounds.

I will make use of what I will call the *Leadership Awareness Onion* to unpack the process...

Peeling the Leadership Onion

To be Become, to change the world, to make the world a better place, etc., to do this or something similar will require us to be acquainted with something I made up called the *Leadership Awareness Onion.* Why that name? Well, for starters, onion is the first item I thought of that has a layered structure. Secondly, the procedure is oftentimes irritating, just like how onions burn and make eyes teary. This just goes to say, it is not going to be easy – a few irritations, burns, or even tears might be endured along the way.

To be fully aware of our leadership capabilities, we have to start by looking at ourselves from the core. And to increase this capability we will have to build layer upon layer, from the core until we can finally change the world.

The core

At the core of this onion is where lies our dormant 'ability to lead', our ability to 'change the world or make it better', 'our potential to grow and become' or whatever you prefer calling it. Within us all, no matter your location, birthplace, background, or current situation, lies a small seed. If watered and adequately taken care of, this seed could grow into something humungous.

This is the starting point: becoming aware and realizing that each and every one of us can change the world if we decide to. But before we change the world, we have to take inventory of that which lies within us. Contrary to the common belief that leaders, high-achievers, world-changers, no-limit-people are born, the *awareness onion* begs to suggest otherwise. It all boils down to what we do with the seed lying at the core. Some may choose to water their seeds seeking growth, while others might keep that seed- that potential as it is.

In the Bible, there is a parable[2] of a man who was travelling to a distant country. Before he left, he entrusted his wealth to his servants:

He gave five bags of silver to one, two bags of silver to another, and one bag of silver to the last—dividing it in proportion to their abilities. He then left on his trip. The servant who received the five bags of silver began to invest the money and earned five more. The servant with two bags of silver also went to work and earned two more. But the servant who received the one bag of silver dug a hole in the ground and hid the master's money.

After a long time, their master returned from his trip and called them to account for how they had used his money. The servant to whom he had entrusted the five bags of silver came forward with five more and said, 'Master, you gave me five bags of silver to invest, and I have earned five more.' The master was full of praise. 'Well done, my good and faithful servant. You have been faithful in handling this small amount, so now I will give you many more responsibilities. Let's celebrate together!

The servant who had received the two bags of silver came forward and said, 'Master, you gave me two bags of silver to invest, and I have earned two more.' The master said, 'Well done, my good and faithful servant. You have been faithful in handling this small amount, so now I will give you many more responsibilities. Let's celebrate together!'

Then the servant with the one bag of silver came and said, 'Master, I knew you were a harsh man, harvesting crops you didn't plant and gathering crops you didn't cultivate. I was afraid I would lose your money, so I hid it in the earth. Look, here is your money back.'

But the master replied, 'You wicked and lazy servant! If you knew I harvested crops I didn't plant and gathered crops I didn't cultivate, why didn't you deposit my money in the bank? At least I could have gotten some interest on it.'

Then he ordered, 'Take the money from this servant and give it to the one with the ten bags of silver. To those who use well what they are given, even more, will be given, and they will have an abundance. But from those who do nothing, even what little they have will be taken away. Now throw this useless servant into outer darkness, where there will be weeping and gnashing of teeth.

It is from the above story that the 'Matthew Principle[3]' is derived. The idea revolves around the premise that those with more will continue getting more. It explains why the gap between the rich and the poor continues to widen – the rich getting richer and the poor getting poorer.

All this to show that those who multiply what they have, will continue amassing more. Those who decide and act towards developing their leadership seeds will continue leading those who don't.

> *'For everyone who has, will more be given, and he will have an abundance.'*

Most of us, unfortunately, are hardwired to think like the third servant. We hide/bury that one talent we have (if we ever get to realize we possess such a talent). With that flawed thought pattern, all we will ever be is potential.

Those who conduct their own autopsy are the ones who will realize what they have within. They are the same ones who will Become and literally change the world. It begins with a choice.

Whether to turn your potential into reality or let it remain as potential. Once you decide to water the seed, then you'll have to grow another layer.

1st Layer: Self-Leadership layer

The 1st layer serves the purpose of protecting your seed, your potential, and talent, and keeps it alive until it can survive as a standalone. Apart from serving as a protective layer for your seed, the first layer can also be thought of as your foundation. Understand this: failure to set up this layer in your life will have a detrimental effect on whether you actually change the world or not.

The reason why 'changing the world' seems somewhat elusive is because those who intend to do so either fail on this first layer or they don't even know that this layer exists.

After that self-autopsy, soon after realizing that you do have the potential/talent to lead, your first project must be the one that addresses self-leadership.

Here is how it works;

1. Realize that you can lead.
2. Lead yourself first.

The leadership journey, dear reader, starts from within before being projected outwards. It is an inside-out sort of a thing. Only after you have self-led you, can you ever hope of leading others and possibly changing the world. That is what Leo Tolstoy[4] meant when he said, *"attend to your own personal development. Everyone thinks of changing the world, but no one thinks of changing himself."*

Self-leadership involves mastering your thinking, your emotions, feelings, habits, and actions. To be able to control these is but a virtue every wannabe-leader must have. Those who have led themselves, attained self-mastery, self-discipline or self-control have had to first peek into their core to see what they have within. They defined themselves – what they could do, and where they could go. They went for it without backing off. The people with this layer of self-leadership are never swayed from their path. They walk the talk; they live what they preach.

Many people miss this. They don't realize that effective, long-lasting, and impactful leadership stems from within. Think about the worlds' greats. What did they have in common? What sort of skill did they have at their disposal to have such impeccable leadership journeys?

Answer: Self-leadership!

They had an inside-out leadership approach. For millions and millions of Indians to follow Gandhi[5] on the passive resistance protests, Gandhi himself showed that he had mastered the art of being at peace. Even after receiving arrests threats and eventually getting assassinated, Martin Luther[6] remained unmoved from fighting against black segregation. It is what he did himself that enabled him to continue leading the masses even from his grave.

Understand this: people rarely act because of what their leader has said, but rather, they act based on what he has done. This is what Ralph Waldo Emerson[7] meant when he said, *'your actions speak so loud – I cannot hear what you are saying.'*

Organizations and big enterprises are no longer looking for the old typical 'managers'; instead, they are looking for leaders. The difference between the two is that one relies on telling people what to do while the other shows his followers how to do it.

If you want to change the world, change yourself – so they say. To most, that sounds clichéd, but this old saying supports the ideology that working on yourself will create ripple effects that will change the world. Once you start working on yourself and watering your seed, when you start nurturing your talents and letting that little light of yours shine - you will inspire action amongst the people around you without even saying a word. Those around you will realize that it's possible, and will be prompted to act on themselves as well. This will set a chain reaction alight, and before you know it, the world will be made a much better place. Made a better place because you decided to lead yourself.

Masters in accumulating power, selling, and negotiating understand this; arguments are easily won through actions rather than the exchange of words. Those who argue through actions have a well-built layer of self-leadership. They have worked thoroughly on themselves. They don't lead through what they say but through what they believe in, which becomes evident by what they do.

You ought to make this your first and most important project. To first find yourself and then conquer yourself. To discipline yourself and listen to yourself, before you can think of leading and conquering someone else. Your actions will speak more than anything you will ever say.

2nd Layer: Leading Others

Once one has managed and passed the level of self-leadership, then without thought, another layer will start to emerge. Unlike the 1st layer of self-leadership, this layer requires relatively less effort to form. In fact, the 2nd layer is a by-product of the 1st layer.

You see, once you make the conscious effort towards self-development and manage to attain a certain level of mastery, you will gain control over your habits and actions and you will manage how you think, handle emotions and feelings. Without conscious effort, you'll find yourself leading others. To lead others is just an automatic yet direct response to succeeding at leading yourself. However, failure to have fully developed the 1st layer of self-leadership makes the forming of the 2nd layer of leading others somewhat harder.

Since we have established that people will be compelled to act by the leader's actions rather than words, to build this 2nd layer, one has to concentrate on the 1st layer.

If you look at the popular religious leaders like Jesus Christ[8], Buddha[9], Muhammad[10], etc. you will notice something peculiar yet similar in nature.

For them to amass the kind of following they had and still have today, they had to do something first. To have had this well-developed ability to lead others, they first had to lead themselves.

Take for instance the story of Siddhartha Gautama:

His life story begins about 2,600 years ago, right around the time he was born in Nepal. Sid (as I will call him) was born into a royal family. He grew up in a very comfortable and luxurious environment. Sid's parents wanted him to be a perfect ruler for their kingdom. So they kept Sid as comfortable as they could and protected him from anything unsatisfactory in the world.

They gave him all the pleasures they could. He was kept in these confines all his life.

When one day he sneaked out to take a tour around the local areas, he was left aghast at what he saw. This was the first time he witnessed suffering. Sid, confronted by this uncomfortable reality that life was not all that rosy, was left upset. This realization, that sickness, ageing, and death was part of life, left him somewhat depressed.

He decided to leave his royal comfort and family in search of life's true meaning. He desperately wanted to feel the pain he had witnessed. He spent the next six years in isolation and lowly places learning how to meditate. Finally, at a place called Bodhgaya, Sid spent six days and nights in deep meditation, neither eating nor moving. Upon attaining the enlightenment he sought, he had a better understanding of life and hence the birth of Buddha, the Awakened One.

After his enlightenment, Sid, now Buddha, journeyed all across India imparting his knowledge with regards to what life was all about. Eventually, he attained a mass following, which led to the emergence of Buddhism.

If you desire to lead men and women, then this should be your starting point. You have to lead yourself first before you can lead others, and once you manage that, then leading others will not be as hard as it seems.

Learn from Sid. He spent years unlocking his own potential. Only when had he unlocked his true potential was he able to bring others to his way of thinking. After Becoming the enlightened one, people didn't need much convincing follow the Buddha.

We definitely have nothing to question about whether or not Buddha changed the world. Of course, he did, and he didn't start by changing it before he changed himself. A similar story can be told of Jesus Christ, Muhammad, etc.

They all embodied what they preached, and for that reason, it didn't take much for them to change the world as they did.

3rd Layer: Changing the world

This layer is arguably the easiest of all layers to form. At face value, of course, it somehow looks like a 'mission impossible' type of a task. While the layer of changing the world is dreaded and perceived by many as a cumbersome task, it is, in actuality, as easy as cutting margarine with a hot knife.

Just to flog a dead horse, you don't just wake up and change the world. Changing the world is a result of firstly changing yourself which inevitably leads to leading and changing others. Changing the world calls for an inside-out approach to leadership.

So then, *Becoming to Lead* is a process that requires us to take a self-introspection first. Followed by self-leadership, then leading others and the effects will cascade to change the world. The beauty in this is that, as you work on Becoming, you unknowingly set yourself on this trajectory of making the world a better place. So, in essence, as you Become, so will you lead and eventually change the world. All because you chose to Become.

When William (The Boy Who Harnessed The Wind) started off, his agenda was just to solve the energy crisis and famine that his family was facing. He did not set out wanting to have an entire village backing him on his ventures or becoming a popular Malawian inventor. But all this and other perks came along with his decision and effort to Become.

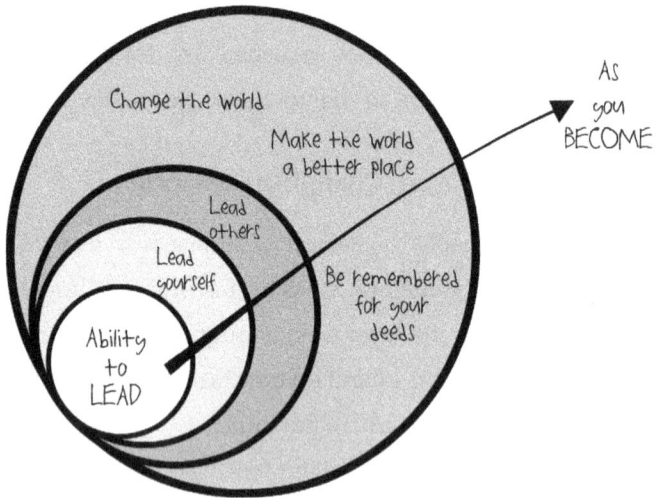

What you will never achieve

A man and his son were once going with their Donkey to a market. As they were walking along by its side, a countryman passed them and said: "You fools, what is a Donkey for, but to ride upon?" So the Man put the Boy on the Donkey, and they went on their way. But soon they passed a group of men, one of whom said: "See that lazy youngster, he lets his father walk while he rides". So the Man ordered his Boy to get off and got on himself. But they hadn't gone far when they passed two women, one of whom said to the other: "Shame on that lazy lout to let his poor little son trudge along." Well, the Man didn't know what to do, but at last, he took his Boy up before him on the Donkey. By this time, they had come to the town, and the passersby began to jeer and point at them. The Man stopped and asked what they were scoffing at. The men said: "Aren't you ashamed of yourself for overloading that poor Donkey of yours—you and your hulking son?" The Man and Boy got off and tried to think of what to do. They thought, and they thought, till at last they cut down a pole, tied the Donkey's feet to it, and raised the pole and the Donkey to their shoulders. They went along amid the laughter of all who met them till they came to Market Bridge, when the Donkey, getting one of his feet loose, kicked out and caused the Boy to drop his end of the pole. In the struggle, the Donkey fell over the bridge, and his fore-feet being tied together, he was drowned.

"That will teach you," said an old man who had followed them: "Please all, and you will please none."

- Aesop's fable[11]

I have had my fair share when it comes to leadership (I think). I have found myself leading in myriad and diverse environments and circumstances. Back in college, I was elected as the Students Union's Secretary General. Not to toot my own horn, but this role I had was a much coveted one. Out of thousands of other students, I was elected to be part of the 15-member team that oversaw all student needs and grievances at my college. I had my ups and downs as I administered the union and sought to unify the student body. Somewhere along the way, I stumbled upon an irrefutable truth. You see, I was at first under the impression that I could meet the needs of every student at my college. My idea of true leadership, throughout my tenure in office, was predicated upon whether or not I could satisfy everyone. However, leading in this environment – full of people of different age groups, sexes, nationalities, and preferences, can be likened to Daedalus' efforts to escape the labyrinth prison.

In retrospect, I realize I was no different from the man journeying to a market with his son and a donkey. Some believed that both the father and son should ride the donkey, some felt it was cruel on the donkey's part and so on.

This is perhaps one of the most valuable lessons I learned in my tenure, and it is something you have to understand before you consider leading. Fact is, as you try to lead and become you will, beyond any reasonable doubt, fail at pleasing or making everyone happy.

Accepting this as an irrefutable law with regards to leadership can be an empowering act one can do for him/herself. Because when we lead most of us assess our effectiveness by the number of people we please. But, the truth of the matter is that, using this as a success metric is a really bad idea.

> *If you want to make everyone happy,*
> *Don't lead*
> *Sell ice cream!*
> *– Unknown*

I know a lot of glorified individuals, both from my community and beyond who have been applauded for their character, integrity, selflessness, etc. In the view of society, they epitomize nobleness and saintliness. Not to sound clichéd, but these people are supposedly perfect, or at least, those around them think so. You probably know a few people who fit this prescribed profile, maybe from your own community, history, or elsewhere.

It is not these individuals that we want to talk about, but rather how these people, no matter how perfect they are perceived to be, they always have opposition and people who don't see their worth in the same light. Whether these individuals are noble or not, is not the question; the point is that nobody has ever managed to please everyone. Nobody has, nobody will (we can bet on that).

In this highly opinionated world we are currently living in, it is impossible not to have someone blurting out and criticizing your efforts and leadership journey. Whatever route or option you choose to take, you are bound to meet grumblings and criticisms because never before in this lifetime has everyone had the same perspective of this world and all its happenings.

In college, I would find myself in dilemmas like how to entertain all the students on campus. A portion of the constituency would prefer a wild party, the other wanted a gospel concert, whilst another called for a sporting event, and so on. Or sometimes, a certain populace of the students would demand that the college tuition should be lowered whilst some thought tuition had to be increased to get quality services. Such instances made me realize that it is impossible to have everyone in one accord. Every decision you make as a leader is bound to be met with some disgruntlements. For every leader – criticism is the way. Like they always they say:

To avoid criticism, do nothing, say nothing, and be nothing

Chapter Summary

Becoming to Lead

Leadership requires an inside-out approach

No-one changes the world without changing him/herself first

Leadership Awareness Onion.

At the core – The ability to lead & change the world (we all have it)

1st layer – Self- Leadership

2nd layer – Leading Others

3rd Layer – Changing the World

What you will never achieve

You will never please everyone.

CHAPTER NINE

BECOMING HAPPY

"If you want to be happy, be."
- Leo Tolstoy.

As we approach the end of this book, I am sure the big question you have is: If I Become, will I be happy? The answer to this thought-provoking question is; IT DEPENDS. This is probably not the most favourable of all responses you would want to hear. But the reason I say it, is that whether Becoming makes us happy or not, is entirely dependent on how we define happiness.

You know what? Before I even try to answer you, let me ask you instead: how much are you willing to pay to be Happy? If you are like most people, or rather like me, my guess is you are willing to play big for happiness. I mean, who doesn't want to be happy? Never in my entire life have I ever met someone who is okay with being miserable and not happy. Everyone is trying, by all means, to be happy.

Happiness is the talk of the moment. Everyone out there is desperately searching for this elusive commodity. I am sure you have heard many people say their goal in life is to be happy (whatever that means). Everybody is busy trying to figure out what that secret ingredient to happiness is. In fact, a whole branch in the psychology field (Positive Psychology[1]) has emerged and flourished, to research and study all there is to happiness. Positive psychology has intimately entertained questions regarding happiness such as what would make a person truly happy? Is it a lot of money? Love and friendships? A happy marriage? A lot of possessions, status, lots of sex, or recognition? Etc.

A lot has been said about what happiness actually is and what it constitutes. However, in working tirelessly on defining what happiness is, few, if any, have taken time to talk about what it is not. Let us be honest, up to now, it is apparent that no one can define what happiness really is. Why not discuss what it is not?

I personally believe that it is equally important to discuss what happiness is not. Because by knowing what happiness is not, we would have eliminated what we would mistake it to be. At least, by knowing what it is not, we will save ourselves from chasing what it appears to be when, in actual fact, it is not.

Let me say it differently:

If we know where happiness is not found, then we will not head in that direction. At least we will have narrowed down the possible locations where happiness might be (not that happiness is located in a particular place).

The Happy Fallacies

I have, and I am sure you also have heard many misconceptions about happiness. The lies that we are told or that we tell ourselves pertaining to the subject of happiness – I want us to discuss just a few of those here. Listed below are the top fallacies regarding happiness that I have come across. I wish it was possible to hear yours as well because there are definitely quite a number of them.

1. With wealth & accolades comes happiness

We all know the story of King Midas[2] who wished for the ability to turn anything he touched into pure gold. Upon receiving this gift, Midas went crazy, turning everything he could get his hands onto, into gold. From chairs to carpets, doors, bathtubs, tables, etc. Everything was rosy and awesome until he got hungry. Upon reaching out and touching an apple, it instantly morphed into gold. The same happened for a grape, a slice of bread, and a glass of water. And, as if that wasn't enough, his beloved daughter tried hugging him and, she too turned into a golden statue!

Just like King Midas, most people believe their happiness lies in gold and/or accolades. For one person, their gold is money, cars, houses, etc. For another its academic achievements, accolades, awards, badges of honour and the likes. Shame on you for judging King Midas for his wish when you are pursuing your gold as well.

We are all hoping that after getting this or that, we are going to be happier. A lot of us are driven by materialistic goals in the pursuit of happiness. After attaining the millionaire title, the Ferrari, or that mansion in the suburbs, I'll be happy, so we think. Just wait till I get that PhD or award you hear them say, only then will I be happier. They don't realize that they are no different from Midas; their goals are gold–driven. In fact, they are worse than Midas because they willingly and knowingly sacrifice everything and everyone for gold.

They miss meals chasing gold and neglect their family's needs in the name of gold. Their eyes are on the gold and nothing else whatsoever. They are running around trading everything for gold because they believe it will make them happier. But somehow, they tend to forget about those who have all they dream of but are still not fulfilled. With all their gold, they are still sad, empty, and alone because they traded everything for gold.

Don't get me wrong. Having all those accolades and wealth isn't bad at all. I don't know about you, but I personally wouldn't mind having a lot of accolades and gold and if you have it, *mazel tov!* If you are working on acquiring such, again, *kudos to you*, my friend. Go for it! However, it becomes problematic when you pursue accolades and gold mistaking them for happiness. Even worse, when you neglect everything and everyone else for gold (turning everything and everyone around you into gold).

No one in their right frame of mind can dispute the fact that having a lot of gold can open doors that were previously closed and give one more freedom and options. However, it is true what they say: *money cannot buy you happiness.* Studies[3] have shown that wealth only matters up to a certain point, and thereafter it will not really have any significant effect on our happiness. And, as concisely put forward by Norrish and Vella-Brodrick[4], *"it has been found that after basic human needs are met, happiness is not clearly associated with wealth or material affluence."* The saying, *'not everything that counts can be counted, and not everything that can be counted counts'*, actually holds water.

In her bestselling book[5], *'Top Five Regrets of the Dying'*, Bronnie Ware gave an account of what people on the brink of death regretted the most. Two of the five regrets were: "I wish I hadn't worked so hard", and "I wish I had stayed in touch with my friends."

This sort of goes against the direction most of us are headed to. Right now, we are working ourselves like donkeys chasing that gold. We are not as connected to our friends as we were because all of us are caught up in our hustles. Only for us to regret at the end of our lives that we didn't spend enough time with our friends, family, and loved ones. It's funny though, how we will regret later when all along, we were substituting and turning them into gold like Midas?

What's rather unfortunate when it comes to gold is that we will never get to a point in our lives where we have acquired enough. We are going to be in need of more of this and that. After a thousand bucks, the aim becomes a million, then a billion, and so on. Just like Midas, we will touch as many items as we can, turning them into gold.

The story of Midas ends on a happy note. All that had been turned into gold through his touch was reversed. But in real life, it doesn't work that way. Now is the time to start doing the things that count.

> *Stop equating your happiness to gold because it is NOT!*

Sure, gold might arouse positive emotions, but ultimately it will never compare to real happiness.

2. Pleasure equals happiness

To be honest, when I first read Bronnie Ware's book: *'The Top Five Regrets of the Dying',* in my mind, I expected something different. I thought, well, probably the dying regretted not drinking enough booze, not getting high on marijuana. I assumed they wished they used a lot of drugs or had a lot of sex (don't you dare judge me!). In my tiny undeveloped mind, I thought that when death was imminent, surely one would regret not having enough pleasure.

Why? Because the commonly shared perspective juxtaposes pleasure to happiness. Pleasure can be somehow equated to happiness, so I thought. Believe it or not, I am not the only one out there who thought this way, and with utmost conviction, a lot more still believe so. The idea that if I seek out pleasure, I will automatically become happy is one that is widely and wildly entertained.

Turns out those who are always on a high – those drowning in pleasure are not as happy as portrayed. In fact, they are the unhappiest of all. The reason they are chasing such highs is to suffocate the negative emotions they inherently have. So the idea is to tune out the negative emotions and not deal with them.

Living life on a high sure sounds pretty amazing. It only does so for a short while before one spirals back into a low. Because that's what pleasure does – it is ecstatic but horribly short-lived. And eventually, pleasure-seeking people get caught up in vicious cycles of chasing highs after highs to maintain that feeling. A brief detachment from the source of pleasure will set those negative emotions loose, and that is the reality they do not want to face.

This is why pleasure doesn't equate to happiness because those undealt with negative emotions will never disappear. They will always be lurking underneath the high waiting to come out when the high-train eventually stops. And it always stops. It is inevitable. You might succeed temporarily to fake happiness by staying on a high, but guess what, *'what goes up must come back down.'*

The constant pursuit of pleasure or living for pleasure is, in actuality, an indicator that one is not happy at all. Those who are indeed happy don't primarily seek pleasure, but pleasure is a by-product of a certain activity.

Quit synonymizing happiness to pleasure because it is NOT!

And, as Aristotle[6] emphasized, *"pleasure is not to be sought for its own sake"*. The moment we seek outright pleasure with the belief that it will make us happy, we would have automatically tasked ourselves with chasing the wind. We might run, momentarily catch up with, and even taste it. But, we cannot run forever, can we?

3. Someone will make me happy.

The belief that happiness is found in another person is not an exotic one. In fact, more people than you could ever imagine presume that their happiness resides in another person. In other words, to be really happy, they have to be with someone, be approved by someone, and be given the actual happiness dose by someone.

You see this commonly in people befriending, associating, dating, or even marrying themselves to certain people, with the presumption that somehow those individuals will make them happy. Their entire existence sort of revolves around those. They want them to approve and reaffirm their beliefs and plans. Or even worse; they want them to make them happy.

For some, their happiness is in their parents. If they are not happy or proud of them, they somehow believe they also cannot be happy. If whatever they do or pursue fails to synchronize with the beliefs or desires they hold for them, they see no possibility whatsoever of attaining happiness.

I am forever appalled by people who actually place their happiness in someone or some people's pockets. We all know how this usually plays out.

Why would you give someone so much power over your life? Your happiness is yours and should stay in your own pocket – not in your lovers' or brothers'. Your happiness should never be predicated on the premise of your social interactions with other people. The ability to make yourself either happy or unhappy should forever remain yours and yours alone.

How someone is going to treat you or see you is in what Steve Covey[7] dubbed *'the sphere of concern'* but unfortunately not in *'the sphere of control'*. That is why I never understand people who say they are with someone because they make them happy. It should never be like that! You should be intrinsically happy, with or without someone. There is a difference between being happy because of someone and being happy to be with someone. Happiness should not be looked for in another person. With or without their love or approval, one should be happy.

If you are with someone because you are seeking happiness, you are in for a treat, my friend. Take heed of Will Smith's[8] wise words, *"her happiness is not my responsibility...Giving someone a responsibility to make you happy when you can't do it for yourself, is selfish"*.

Funny how we do that all the time. Hoping and expecting someone or some people will make us happy.

It is your job to make you happy

If you are waiting to be approved of by your family to be happy, you are in trouble. Yes, family should mean so much to you, but bestowing on them such power towards your happiness is a little too extreme. There is no guarantee that you will continue seeing eye-to-eye, sharing the same beliefs and value systems. And just to be safe – keep your happiness in your own pocket, not in your father's or wife's.

4. If I go there, I'll be happy

There is a trend that is spreading like wildfire. Everywhere you look, people are talking about it. The idea of travelling across the globe is one that is being romanticized at the moment. Everyone seems to be globetrotting like never before, and they claim to be happier than before.

We hear stories of people who woke up one day bored and sick of what they were doing. They held an auction, sold all their possessions, packed their backpacks, bought a one–way plane ticket, and journeyed to the other end of the planet in search of Nirvana[9]. They set up Blogs, and Youtube accounts to glorify vagabonding. They continuously bombard the internet with their Aha-Moments, thrills, and stories. Now more than ever, many people are being sold on this idea of trekking the globe.

Back in the day, our ancestors believed that the earth was flat, and if one wandered off too far, he/she would fall off the edge into some abyss. And since the day we discovered that our ancestors were wrong about this, we became entranced with this nomadic mindset. And, what better way is there to sell travelling than attaching it to happiness?

For many, the *'pot of gold at the end of the rainbow'* myth is held dearly and believed. Well, maybe not in the literal sense, but many people now believe that their happiness is tied to someplace or destination. That is, to be happy – they have to be free as a bird and fly over the horizon to someplace full of fresh air and clear waters. I mean, why not? The internet is full of people who got their 'pots of gold' halfway across the globe.

No one can dispute the pros that come along with travelling. Certainly, there is so much to be gained like growth, breaking cycles, gaining clarity, de-stressing, etc. If one can, they should definitely travel. If given the opportunity, I would too. But to posit that travelling will make someone happier than they already are is, in my own perspective, not true.

The prospect of quitting your job, selling all your stuff, and going someplace no one knows you can be exhilarating. But, that's where the problem is; excitement and thrill, just like pleasure is not happiness and it is short-lived. It might last longer for some, but it certainly won't last forever. Your happiness is not tied to a place or a destination other than inside of you.

At the end of the day, who you are on the inside (happy or sad) will not change because you changed your geographical location. Either you are happy, or you are not. If you are about to sell all your stuff to seek happiness in someplace, I am glad I got to you before you did so. Stop!

> *The only happiness you get. Is the happiness you go with.*

Imagine after six months you come back cowering, broke, lonely, homeless and above all, not-so-happy and as sad as before you left. However, if you are travelling for the thrill, excitement, growth, to de-stress, etc., then go ahead. Just don't expect happiness because it is not in a place. You can be happy right where you are if you choose to be.

The Hedonic Treadmill

Think about that time when you were really excited about getting something. Maybe it was the day before you finally got the latest iPhone or MacBook. The day she finally said yes to going on a date with you or even marrying you. That day you got your degree, medal or that recognition. Maybe it is the day you bought your dream car or moved to your new house in your favourite town. It could be that day your passport, visa and plane ticket were all in one place ready for that trip. Think about these or other similar moments.

Do you remember how exhilarated you were? How joy coursed throughout your entire body in a never-ending fashion? What a memory, right? The best feeling ever!

Let us imagine even further....

After attaining that phone, lover, house, car, etc. chances are that spike in exhilaration took a dip afterwards. You got used to the phone, we forgot how beautiful the new house was and the car just became another car in our garage.

What happened to the excitement? How is it that all of a sudden after finally putting our hands on the items we yearned for so much, the level of excitement waned? After putting our hands on the elusive *'pot of gold at the end of the rainbow'* – what happened? At one point, we were convinced that getting this or that was going to make us super-duper-happy. We experienced happiness-on-steroids when we were an inch away from our goal. But the happiness turned out to be short-lived as soon as we acquired it.

Was it because the goal was not what we thought it was?

No, I personally do not think so. That goal - the item you were seeking was worth it, and the sudden lack of thrill towards it has less to do with the actual goal and more to do with the human make-up.

The real cause of this experience or cycle is what the psychologists have termed: *The Hedonic Treadmill*[10] or the *Hedonic Adaptation Theory*. The concept suggests that we (all of us) tend to return to our baseline level of happiness despite what we acquire or go through. That's what I have been trying to iterate through *The Happy Fallacies*. Even if you get this or that – it will not do much towards your level of happiness. At least in the long run.

What fascinates me further is the fact that the Hedonic Treadmill also applies to adverse situations. Even when we go through negative circumstances, we might only be saddened for a while. Still, with time we will eventually find ourselves as happy as before that bad thing happened to us. Do you remember that time you were heartbroken, when you were backstabbed, lost a loved one, your car destroyed in an accident? Or that other time, when you lost your job or you were robbed of your priceless possessions? Chances are, when you experienced that unfavourable circumstance, your entire world shattered. For a brief moment a dark cloud hung over you, and you didn't see any possible chance of surviving that storm.

But look at you now...

What changed? Is it because the passing of your loved one does not matter anymore? Of course not! Through Hedonic Treadmill, your happiness, even though it took a dip, naturally and gradually rose back to its baseline level.

Research carried out by Brickman and Campbell[11] in 1971, studied two groups of people towards ascertaining this concept. One group was made up of those who had just won the lottery while the other was mostly made up of accident victims (most of them on crutches and wheelchairs). What they found out later when these groups were again looked at in 1978 was that ultimately both the lotto winners and the accident victims appeared to be equally happy. From the two groups, none seemed to be happier than the other. In our minds, we would think that lotto winners were probably happier, while the accident victims were miserable. But, that's not the case because their happiness baselines remained fairly the same. Despite the initial increase/decrease in the levels of happiness, they all returned to their original state.

THE HEDONIC TREADMILL GRAPH

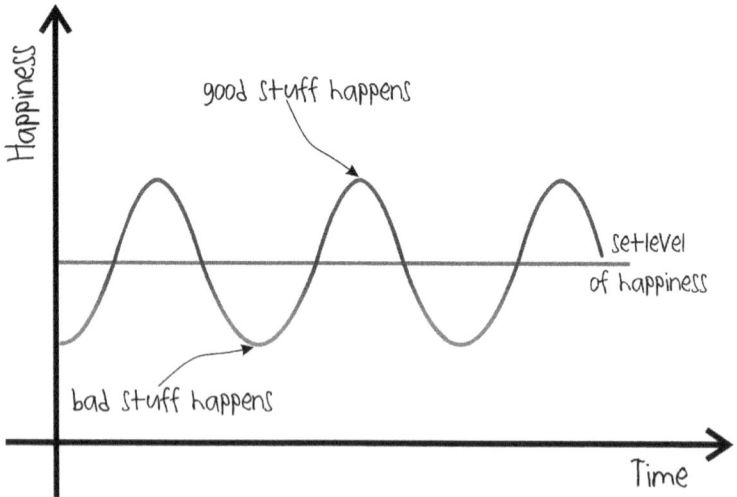

You probably doubted *The Happy Fallacies.* You thought that I was wrong to suggest that neither money, accolades, pleasure, people, nor places would make you any happier than you already are. I hope you have seen where I am coming from.

Despite what happens to us (good or bad), our happiness is barely affected or changed as much as we tend to assume. Getting the car, the girl, award, feeling the pleasure, or even going to our dream country will elate us in that moment, but with adaptation, the thrill will falter, and we will be as happy or sad as we were before any of that happened.

Beyond the Treadmill

When I first encountered *The Hedonic Treadmill Theory*, I couldn't help but wonder: *"If there is an already made level of happiness, what is the point in doing anything?"* I am sure you are also wondering the same thing. This concept of having a preset happiness baseline seems to posit that no matter what you do in your life, you will never become happier or sadder than you already are. Like you are born happy or sad, and that's it. Right?

Well, partially, it's true, happiness has been linked with our genes. Lucky for us, Ed Diener, further researched this concept and debunked some grey areas including this issue of the happiness baseline. In his study[12], *Beyond the Hedonic Treadmill*, he shed more light on the baseline and other overlooked issues.

In his revision, he laid out five key points listed as follows:

1. Baselines are not neutral.

More recent studies disagree with the *Hedonic Treadmill* concept when it suggests that people, after every situation, always revert back to a neutral point. A neutral position meaning one is neither happy nor sad. Or half sad, half happy.

The research found that people are generally happy most of the time. That is, naturally, people are inclined to be more happy than sad. Eighty percent of the respondents from a study of diverse populations like the Amish, African Maasai, etc. claimed to be quite happy.

So, no matter what people go through, they will indeed return to a baseline, however it will not be a neutral one but rather a positive one. That is a relief, right? That even though genetic make-up, to some extent, comes into play towards happiness, we are all naturally happier than we are sad.

2. Baselines are not the same.

Another weakness or misleading fact about *The Hedonic Treadmill* is that it tends to suggest that we all have the same level of happiness. But, this is not true – the happiness baselines are variegated and differ from one person to another. This is pretty obvious to be fair. Some people are naturally more inclined to be happier more than others.

Every person has his/her own happiness baseline level. Their personality traits partially influence the variation of these baselines. In other words, your well-being has so much to do with your perspective. It's about how you view and interpret the happenings of this world.

And, in some way as mentioned before, happiness has been found to be heritable to some extent. This was shown through research and the study[13] of identical twins. The study showed that even if they were raised apart from each other and in different environments, they would report having the same level of well-being. While that was not the case for 'Non Identical Twins.'

3. A person has multiple baselines.

If you ask me, recent studies have further complicated the *Hedonic Adaptation Theory.* Diener and colleagues, also argued that we could not treat well-being as a single entity guided by a singular baseline. Instead, happiness constitutes a whole lot of other factors that ultimately build up to our well-being. Sometimes, one area might be facing a positive change, while another one is being negatively affected.

In essence, in the professional space, you might be making notable strides, getting promoted, and salary raises while at the same time, your marriage is falling apart. To say you are happy or unhappy would not cover it, because your work satisfaction is on an all-high, but your marital satisfaction is on a low.

Both your work and marriage add up towards your well-being, but clearly, they are operating exclusively. They don't share the same baseline.

4. Happiness levels can change.

Probably this is what's worrying about this concept: does it mean we can never be happier or unhappier than we already are?

A 2005 study carried[14] out by Fujita and Diener for 17 years in Germany showed that happiness levels are not cemented and final. Over time it is possible to become or feel happier. As Martin Seligman posited, *"The very good news is there is quite a number of internal circumstances . . . under your voluntary control. If you decide to change them (none of these changes come without real effort), your level of happiness is likely to increase lastingly."*

Happiness is indeed an internal circumstance that forever remains in our control. With the right amount of effort and calibration, we can increase it.

5. Adaptation is not the same.

Another of The Hedonic concept's weaknesses is that it tends to suggest that, when faced with either a positive or negative situation, we will all adapt to it in a similar fashion.

Someone's great news, to another, is just news. When Lucas[15] looked into the effects of marriage on individuals' levels of happiness, he found something rather appalling.

Those who seemed happy before marrying did not report to be any happier after marrying. There was no huge difference in the levels of happiness before and after marriage. On the other hand, those who were unhappy before marriage tended to believe they were a lot happier than they were before marriage. Those who were less satisfied before marriage benefited from this one positive situation, and it significantly moved their baselines as compared to those who were more satisfied prior to marriage.

With every situation that comes our way, be it positive or negative – we are hit differently. Buying a car when one already has a garage full of cars will affect him/her differently from one who has just bought his/her first car.

Stepping off the Treadmill

Literally speaking, the thing I hate the most about being on a treadmill is that no matter how hard or how long I run, I will never actually get anywhere. I could run for days – nonstop, and even if the screen reflected thousands of kilometres covered, I will still be in the same room.

That is exactly what happens in real life. If you are chasing happiness in the form of some wealth and accolades, pleasure, in people, or a place, then you are on a very deadly treadmill. No matter how much money you acquire, or the pleasure you seek and find. Or, the people that come into your life or the places you go to -unfortunately, none will give you happiness.

As the Hedonic Adaptation Theory has laid it out, our happiness will emanate from our personality traits and slightly from our genetic makeup. The money, pleasure, people, places, etc. might excite us for a moment or two, but we will always find ourselves feeling how we always felt before we had those things.

I will repeat this: it would be cool to have it all, but to seek those under the assumption that I am going to be happy is a really bad idea.

Now is the time to stop looking for happiness out there in other people or materialistic possessions and start looking for happiness inside of yourself. What needs our attention is not the ups and downs of the curved line, but the baseline. This is because the ups and downs are affected by external factors that we barely have control over while the baseline is only affected by the internal factors.

Our backstabbing friend can temporarily cause us to feel hurt and unhappy, but over time, we will be back at our normal selves (at our baselines). In essence, we are happy because we are happy or sad because we are sad. We are neither happy nor sad because of what happens to us; instead, we are happy or sad despite what happens to us.

What is important is that we expend most of our energy on raising the baseline to a higher level than it currently is. The baseline is the only thing we can influence.

Remember the concept of Ikigai discussed in Chapter 5? The idea that happiness and wellbeing are found at the intersection of doing what the world needs, what you are good at, what you love, and what you can get paid for? I could not think of anything else that could bring us closer to being happy than *Ikigai*. The beauty of practicing this ancient Japanese art is that it puts us on a never-ending journey of seeking something bigger than our current selves. It diverts our attention from the results to the actual journey, and at any point in our life, we can find a lot to be happy about. And, even when we go through adversity, we never lose sight of the bigger picture. The bigger picture being the baseline.

In continually trying to serve the world, doing what we love, aiming to become an expert at it, and making money out of it - we will be raising our baselines. The idea is to balance the four.

Over and above, we need to think of progress in terms of our baselines to increase our wellbeing. No matter how minute, over time, every slight effort put towards raising our baselines will go a long way towards our wellbeing and ultimately towards our happiness.

In my own opinion, growth and intrinsic progress are what will make us happy. But hey, don't take my word for it – find out for yourself what makes you happy, but at least I have told you what most people confuse it with. However, if we are in agreement that indeed, internal personal growth will make us happier in the long run, then we have our answer.

The question was: will you be happier if you Become?

Yes, and yes! Nothing speaks about personal mastery, personal discipline, growth, or internal victory more than Becoming. I have no shred of doubt in my mind that Becoming will go a long way towards your wellbeing and happiness. For a genuinely Become person, happiness will not be elusive because it will be inside them and not externalized.

A Becomer is one with a well-oiled mind in terms of perspective. His or Her happiness is not attached to a bank account, some person, achievements, places, pleasure, etc. It is more internal than it is external.

JUST BE HAPPY!

On Happiness:
The only happiness you get;
Is the happiness you bring.
Nothing more!
Nothing less!

Chapter Summary

Becoming Happy

The Happy Fallacies
Happiness is in wealth and accolades
Pleasure equals Happiness
Someone can make me happy
If I go to that place I'll be happy

The Hedonic Treadmill
Your happiness has less to do with what you achieve or experience on the outside.

Stepping off the treadmill
Focus on personal intrinsic growth

CHAPTER TEN

THE ART OF BECOMING

"For me, becoming isn't about arriving somewhere or achieving a certain aim. I see it instead as forward motion, a means of evolving, a way to reach continuously toward a better self. The journey doesn't end."

– Michelle Obama

Captain Becoming

Let me introduce you to the baddest and toughest guy on this whole planet, you have probably not even heard of.

Captain Becoming!

I know in your mind, you are probably thinking of Captain America[1]. But, Captain America has nothing compared to this guy. In fact, the entire Avengers Marvel[2] squad can't beat this guy in any way.

Our super invincible being has something none of the other fictional heroes have. You might be wondering, what makes our guy special. Captain B, as I will call him, has an impressive ability to pursue anything he sets his mind to, despite his physical makeup or current limitations. Even if he was to be blind like Hein Wagner[3] or old, like Lena Salmi[4], this guy would go out and seek whatever he desired.

However, he does not consider himself special in any way. In fact his favorite mantra is, *'Nobody is superior, nobody is inferior, and nobody is equal either. People are simply unique and incomparable'.*

This god-like person understands and is guided by Three Laws:

1. He knows that for circumstances to change for the better in his life, he has to act.
2. Captain B is also cognizant that change is affected by the effort put towards it and the size of that desired change.
3. Finally, he understands and believes that actions have equal and opposite reactions.

To avoid procrastinating or putting his plans off, Cap rewards himself for every baby step he takes in the right direction. He also makes use of accountability partners, and he publicly announces his plans. He commits irreversibly and incentivises all his efforts. He also aligns all his beliefs to his behaviours and he always acts, regardless of the fact that he is motivated or not.

Unlike the other superheroes, Captain Becoming is no immortal. He has come to terms with the fact that death is inevitable and has learned to value life ever since. He expends his energy and time only on that which feeds his soul. Ultimately his major goal is to leave the world a much better place than it was before he passed through. Most importantly, he gives the world all that he has – because he knows that there will only be one version of him.

Captain B is good at "trusting the process" – taking only one step at a time, and to him, that is more than enough. He is willing to forgo instant gratification for long term benefit. He is not in any competition with anyone but only himself.

Captain B is a stupendous adversity absorber. That is, he is never phased by any form of adversity, be it mistakes, rejections, losses, betrayals, or criticism. He can somehow turn every negative situation that comes his way into an advantage.

He remains forever-focused on changing himself for the better before trying to change others or the world. In essence; he leads from within.

Finally, Captain Becoming is the happiest person you will ever meet. He does not seek happiness in pleasure, accolades, in places or people. What makes Cap happy is intrinsic personal growth and not any external validation.

In other words, in, Becoming, he is happier.

What a remarkable super-human. Right?

What if I were to tell you that this fictional-like being exists?

YOU are Captain Becoming. Well, let me put it this way: YOU COULD BE Captain B if you chose to.

You could be your very own Captain Becoming. And, of course, to be a Captain Becoming, all you need to do is to...................... BECOME!

Become today, Become tomorrow, Become next month, next year, and continue Becoming for as long as you are still breathing.

Keep Becoming and be an unstoppable super-human.

Cheers! Captain Becoming

EPILOGUE

Funny! Where I was when I started writing this book and where I am today are totally different worlds. The process of writing this book, the commitment, the research, the collaborations and friendships forged have greatly affected me in a positive way. I feel more alive and more connected than ever and most of all I think I am happy with where I am headed to.

I feel like I am Becoming (I believe I am)

I sincerely hope that this book did to you what it did for me, or even better. I hope it helped you to get closer towards Becoming!

However, I want you to remember these words;

"For me,
Becoming isn't about arriving somewhere or achieving a certain aim.
I see it instead as forward motion, a means of evolving, a way to reach continuously toward a better self.
The journey doesn't end."

– Michelle Obama
(Author of the book: Becoming)

It would be delusional of me to think that I have exhausted all there is about "next level". I just started a conversation that we need to keep ablaze.

Best of luck on your journey.
See you on the other side.
Yours In Becoming
Ruramai Sithole

ACKNOWLEDGEMENTS

If I have seen further, it is by standing on the shoulders of giants.
- Sir Isaac Newton, 1676

TO BE HONEST, I don't think I would have managed to see this book project through without some divine intervention. I want to thank the Lord Almighty for allowing me to pursue and finish such a project. I believe it is through the Holy Spirit that I had good health, big ideas and enough strength.

So many people took part in the creation of this book.

Before anyone else, I must thank my girlfriend, Lisa, who played a pivotal role throughout this process. She hates reading, but she read my manuscript countless times. Not to mention the emotional support she gave me when my writing days were dark and gloomy.

Secondly, I am grateful to my family; I consider them my biggest and most loyal fans. Their support and encouragement is indispensable. I must say the way they believe in me is sometimes more than the belief I have in myself. Special mention goes to my sister, Rutendo. She is a rockstar, and her effort towards making this book a success is priceless.

Thirdly, to Kim Hunter, for turning my messy manuscript into an actual readable book. I am awestruck, and I appreciate the patience she had on me.

As for the cover and interior design of the book, I cannot put in words how much I salute Tendai Chidziya's delicate touch. I am impressed by not only his creativity but his ability to separate friendship from business.

At various stages of writing, I benefited from the guidance of my mentor/friend/colleague (I honestly don't know how to classify her). Thanks to Barbara K Nyathi for walking this journey with me. I can't think of anyone who would have done it better than you.

I want to thank the many people who constantly asked me questions like "How's the book going?" "When will it be ready?" etc. Questions like these kept me going when I felt like slacking or putting it off. Without you guys, I would have procrastinated on this project. Thank you: Leigh Joy Mansel-Pleydell, Pahukeni Kangayi, Michael C. Mayumbula, Hermien Elago, Rufaro S Matare, Trustworth Mandinyenya, Leeroy T Mudengezi, Tinashe Muzata, Kumbirai T Chifamba, Tafadzwa Musundire, Tafadzwa Mpundu, Talent Matema, and Brian Tholanah.

I am certain there are people I have probably left out (unintentionally). Please forgive me. Just let me know, and I will add you onto my master list of the people who have played a role in my way of thinking and life as a whole.

The full list can be found at:

https://ruramaisithole.com/my-titans/.

And finally, I want to acknowledge you, dear reader, for taking this journey of Becoming with me, for investing your precious time and money on this book.

Thank you!

I hope you BECOME!

November 2020

MEET THE AUTHOR

RURAMAI is a Speaker and Author who is all about the 'next level.' When he speaks or writes, the intention is always to build men and women to step into their 'next level.'

It is his utmost purpose through his work to inspire and motivate people to be their best selves.

Find out more about the Author at:

https://ruramaisithole.com/

Read with Me

THANK YOU SO much for taking the time to read this book. I hope there was an appreciable return on the time and financial investment you made on this book.

If you enjoyed *If We Are To Become*, then you may like my other writing as well.

You can read my articles at:

https://ruramaisithole.com/articles/

I also send out a free Monday Motivation (#MoMo) newsletter, and you can sign up at:

https://ruramaisithole.com/newsletter/

In addition to my own work, I also send out a reading list of my favourite books from other authors on a wide range of subjects.

See here at:

https://ruramaisithole.com/reading-list/

Subscribers are also the first to hear about my newest articles, books, events and projects.

NOTES

In this section, I have incorporated a rundown of notes, references, and citations for every part in the book. I may have committed an error someplace in this book— in not offering credit to somebody where it is expected. If this is so, please email me at becoming@ruramaisithole.com so I can fix the issue at the earliest opportunity.

Prologue

1. Zimbabwe

"Officially the Republic of Zimbabwe, formerly Rhodesia, is a landlocked country located in Southern Africa, between the Zambezi and Limpopo Rivers, bordered by South Africa, Botswana, Zambia, and Mozambique. The capital and largest city is Harare. The second-largest city is Bulawayo. A country of roughly 14 million people, Zimbabwe has 16 official languages, with English, Shona, and Ndebele, the most common."
Wikipedia, 2020. Wikipedia. [Online]
Available at: https://en.wikipedia.org/wiki/Zimbabwe

2. Matt Haig (Wikipedia, 2020)

http://www.matthaig.com/
"Matt Haig (born 3 July 1975) is an English novelist and journalist. He has written both fiction and non-fiction for children and adults, often in the speculative fiction genre. Haig is the author of both fiction and non-fiction for children and adults. His work of non-fiction, Reasons to Stay Alive, was a number one Sunday Times bestseller and was in the UK top 10 for 46 weeks."
Wikipedia, 2020. Wikipedia. [Online]
Available at: https://en.wikipedia.org/wiki/Matt_Haig

Chapter 1: Becoming

1. Hein Wagner

https://www.heinwagner.com/

2. Video

Wagner, H., 2009. blindmanwithvision. [Online]
Available at: https://www.youtube.com/watch?v=j5EFNmk8tfw

3. Lewis Hamilton

https://www.lewishamilton.com/
Lewis Carl Davidson Hamilton (born 7 January 1985) is a British racing driver who

races in Formula One for the Mercedes-AMG Petronas Formula One Team. A six-time Formula One World Champion, he is widely regarded as one of the greatest drivers in the history of the sport and considered by some to be the greatest of all time.

Wikipedia, 2020. Wikipedia. [Online]
Available at: https://en.wikipedia.org/wiki/Lewis_Hamilton

4. Lena Salmi

Available at: https://www.youtube.com/watch?v=IJ8A42UXeck
Gill, N., 2018. Hypebae. [Online]
Available at: https://hypebae.com/2018/2/lena-very-old-skateboarders-interview
Anon., n.d. Heart. [Online]
Available at: https://www.heart.co.uk/lifestyle/older-ladies-prove-age-is-a-number-inspirational/

5. Johanna Quaas

Johanna Quaas (born 20 November 1925 in Hohenmölsen) is a German gymnast. As of 2018, she is the oldest gymnast in the world. Quaas is a regular competitor in the amateur competition Landes-Seniorenspiele, staged in Saxony, Germany.

Wikipedia, 2020. Wikipedia. [Online]
Available at: https://en.wikipedia.org/wiki/Johanna_Quaas

6. Jean Harcourt

An 85-year-old marathon runner.

Day, R., 2018. Manchester Evening News. [Online]
Available at: https://www.manchestereveningnews.co.uk/news/greater-manchester-news/great-grandma-getting-ready-run-14301972

7. William Kamkwamba

William Kamkwamba, B. M., 2009. The Boy Who Harnessed the Wind: Creating currents of electricity and hope. 1st ed. s.l.: HarperCollins e-books.
The Boy Who Harnessed the Wind. 2019. [Film] Directed by Chiwetel Ejiofor. United Kingdom; Malawi: Participant Media; BBC Films; British Film Institute.

8. Using Energy

Atwater, M., 1995. Using Energy. 1st ed. s.l.: Macmillan McGraw-Hill.

9. Ernest Hemmingway (Wikipedia, 2020)

Ernest Miller Hemingway (21 July 1899 – 2 July 1961) was an American journalist, novelist, short-story writer, and sportsman. His economical and understated style—which he termed the iceberg theory—had a strong influence on 20th-century fiction, while his adventurous lifestyle and his public image brought him admiration from later generations. Hemingway produced most of his work between the mid-1920s and the mid-1950s, and he won the Nobel Prize in Literature in 1954. Many of his works are considered classics of American literature.

10. Robin Sharma

Sharma, R., 2006. The Greatness Guide: Powerful Secrets for Getting to World Class. 2nd ed. s.l.: Harper Business.

11. Vasco Da Gama

Vasco da Gama was a Portuguese explorer and the first European to reach India by sea.

His initial voyage to India (1497–1499) was the first to link Europe and Asia by an ocean route, connecting the Atlantic and the Indian oceans and, therefore, the West and the Orient. This is widely considered a milestone in world history, as it marked the beginning of a sea-based phase of global multiculturalism.

Wikipedia, 2020. Wikipedia. [Online]

Available at: https://en.wikipedia.org/wiki/Vasco_da_Gama

Chapter 2: The Truth

1. Martin Seligman

Martin Elias Pete Seligman (born August 12, 1942) is an American psychologist, educator, and author of self-help books. Seligman is a strong promoter within the scientific community of his theories of positive psychology and of well-being. His theory of learned helplessness is popular among scientific and clinical psychologists. A Review of General Psychology survey, published in 2002, ranked Seligman as the 31st most cited psychologist of the 20th century.

2. Learned helplessness theory

Learned helplessness is a behaviour exhibited by a subject after enduring repeated aversive stimuli beyond their control. It is thought to be caused by the subject's acceptance of their powerlessness: discontinuing attempts to escape or avoid the aversive stimulus, even when such alternatives are unambiguously presented. Upon exhibiting such behaviour, the subject was said to have acquired learned helplessness.

Seligman, M. E. P., 1975. Helplessness. On depression, development, and death. 1st ed. s.l.: W. H. Freeman.

Wikipedia, 2020. Wikipedia. [Online]

Available at: https://en.wikipedia.org/wiki/Learned_helplessness

3. Donald Hiroto

Hiroto, D. S. Locus of control and learned helplessness. Journal of Experimental Psychology, 1974, 102, 187-193.

Hiroto, D. S. and Seligman, M. E. P. Generality of learned helplessness in man. Journal of Personality and Social Psychology, 1974, in press.

4. The boy who flew too close to the sun

Farmer, P., 1971. Daedalus and Icarus. 1st ed. s.l.: Harcourt Brace Jovanovich, Inc.

5. Captain America

Captain America is a superhero appearing in American comic books published by Marvel Comics. Captain America was designed as a patriotic supersoldier

Wikipedia, 2020. Wikipedia. [Online]
Available at: https://en.wikipedia.org/wiki/Captain_America

6. Robert Greene
Greene, R., 2018. Know your limits: The law of grandiosity. In: The laws of human nature. s.l.: Profile Books, pp. 292 -319.

7. Jocko Willink
Willink, J. & Babin, L., 2017. Check the ego. In: 2nd, ed. Extreme Ownership. s.l.: St Martin's Press, p. 100.

8. Eckhart Tolle. (Wikipedia, 2020)
Eckhart Tolle (February 16, 1948) is a spiritual teacher and best-selling author. He is a German-born resident of Canada. He is best known as the author of The Power of Now and A New Earth: Awakening to Your Life's Purpose. In 2008, The New York Times called Tolle "the most popular spiritual author in the United States"
https://eckharttolle.com/
Wikipedia, 2020. Wikipedia. [Online]
Available at: https://en.wikipedia.org/wiki/Eckhart_Tolle

9. Mark Manson -"You are not special"
Manson, M., 2016. You are not special. In: The subtle art of not giving a f*uck. 1st ed. s.l.: HarperOne.

Chapter 3: Newton Laws of Becoming
1. Sir Isaac Newton
(1642 – 1727) was an English mathematician, physicist, astronomer, theologian, and author who is widely recognised as one of the most influential scientists of all time and as a key figure in the scientific revolution.
Wikipedia, 2020. Wikipedia. [Online]
Available at: https://en.wikipedia.org/wiki/Isaac_Newton

2. Newton's laws of motion
Are three physical laws that, together, laid the foundation for classical mechanics. They describe the relationship between a body and the forces acting upon it, and its motion in response to those forces. These three laws have been expressed in several ways, over nearly three centuries, and can be summarised as follows:
First law
In an inertial frame of reference, an object either remains at rest or continues to move at a constant velocity, unless acted upon by a force.
Second law
In an inertial frame of reference, the vector sum of the forces F on an object is equal to the mass m of that object multiplied by the acceleration a of the object: $F = ma$. (It is assumed here that the mass m is constant)
Third law
When one body exerts a force on a second body, the second body simultaneously

exerts a force equal in magnitude and opposite in direction on the first body.
Wikipedia, 2020. Wikipedia. [Online]
Available at: https://en.wikipedia.org/wiki/Newton%27s_laws_of_motion

3. You reap what you sow.

Anon., n.d. Galatians 6: 7. In: The Holy Bible. s.l.:s.n.

4. John Cena

John Felix Anthony Cena Jr. (born 23 April 1977) is an American professional wrestler, actor, rapper, and television presenter.
Wikipedia, 2020. Wikipedia. [Online]
Available at: https://en.wikipedia.org/wiki/John_cena

5. Dwayne The Rock Johnson

Dwayne Douglas Johnson (born 2 May 1972), also known by his ring name The Rock, is an American-Canadian actor, producer, businessman, retired professional wrestler, and former American football player. He wrestled for the World Wrestling Federation (WWF, now WWE) for eight years before pursuing an acting career.
Wikipedia, 2020. Wikipedia. [Online]
Available at: https://en.wikipedia.org/wiki/Dwayne_Johnson

6. Lionel Andrés Messi Cuccittini

(born 24 June 1987) is an Argentine professional footballer who plays as a forward and captains both Spanish club Barcelona and the Argentina national team. Often considered the best player in the world and widely regarded as one of the greatest players of all time.
Wikipedia, 2020. Wikipedia. [Online]
Available at: https://en.wikipedia.org/wiki/Lionel_Messi

7. Christiano Ronaldo

Cristiano Ronaldo dos Santos Aveiro (born 5 February 1985) is a Portuguese professional footballer who plays as a forward for Serie A club Juventus and captains the Portugal national team. Often considered the best player in the world and widely regarded as one of the greatest players of all time
Wikipedia, 2020. Wikipedia. [Online]
Available at: https://en.wikipedia.org/wiki/Cristiano_Ronaldo

8. Stephen Curry

Wardell Stephen "Steph" Curry II (14 March 1988) is an American professional basketball player for the Golden State Warriors of the National Basketball Association (NBA). A six-time NBA All-Star, Curry has been named the NBA Most Valuable Player (MVP) twice and won three NBA championships with the Warriors. Many players and analysts have called him the greatest shooter in NBA history
Wikipedia, 2020. Wikipedia. [Online]
Available at: https://en.wikipedia.org/wiki/Stephen_Curry

9. LeBron Raymone James Sr.

(born 30 December 1984) is an American professional basketball player for the Los Angeles Lakers of the National Basketball Association (NBA). He is widely considered to be one of the greatest basketball players in NBA history. Discussions ranking him as the greatest basketball player of all time have often been subject to significant debate, with frequent comparisons to Michael Jordan. James's teams have played in eight consecutive NBA Finals (2011–2018 seasons) between the Miami Heat and Cleveland Cavaliers.

Wikipedia, 2020. Wikipedia. [Online]

Available at: https://en.wikipedia.org/wiki/LeBron_James

10. James Edward Harden Jr.

(born 26 August 1989) is an American professional basketball player for the Houston Rockets of the National Basketball Association (NBA).

Wikipedia, 2020. Wikipedia. [Online]

Available at: https://en.wikipedia.org/wiki/James_Harden

11. Robert Greene (Greene, 2000) Law 32 of Power

Greene, R., 2000. The 48 Laws of Power. 1st ed. s.l.: Profile Books.

12. Steve Covey

Covey, S. R., 2017. The 7 Habits of Highly Effective People. 1st ed. s.l.: FranklinCovey Co.

13. "Karma Effect"

Lee, C., 2018. Medium. [Online]

Available at: https://medium.com/@chengeerlee/karma-the-universal-law-of-cause-and-effect-32e21621d4c4

Mendel, B., n.d. Mindworks. [Online]

Available at: https://mindworks.org/blog/understanding-karma-cause-effect-2/

14. Reverse engineering

Also called back engineering, is the process by which a man-made object is deconstructed to reveal its designs, architecture, or code. Reverse engineering is applicable in the fields of computer engineering, mechanical engineering, and electronic engineering, software engineering, chemical engineering, and systems biology.

Wikipedia, 2020. Wikipedia. [Online]

Available at: https://en.wikipedia.org/wiki/Reverse_engineering

15. Cause and effect

(also referred to as causation, or Causality) is influence by which one event, process or state (a cause) contributes to the production of another event, process or state (an effect) where the cause is partly responsible for the effect, and the effect is partly dependent on the cause.

Goldstein, J., 2008. Tricycle. [Online]

Available at: https://tricycle.org/magazine/cause-and-effect/
Wikipedia, 2020. Wikipedia. [Online]
Available at: https://en.wikipedia.org/wiki/Causality

Chapter 4: To avoid not doing

1. Classical Conditioning & 2. Operant conditioning.
Nevid, J. S., 2007. Learning. In: 2nd, ed. Psychology concept and applications. s.l.: Houghton Mifflin, pp. 182-207.

3. Burrhus Frederic Skinner
(20 March 1904 – 18 August 1990) was an American psychologist, behaviourist, author, inventor, and social philosopher.[2][3][4][5] He was the Professor of Psychology at Harvard University from 1958 until his retirement in 1974
Hunt, M., 1993. The story of psychology. 1st ed. s.l.: Anchor Books.
Wikipedia, 2020. Wikipedia. [Online]
Available at: https://en.wikipedia.org/wiki/B._F._Skinner

4. Abraham Maslow
Maslow, A., 2019. A Theory of Human Motivation. 1st ed. s.l.: General Press.

5. Army general and his men
Sharma, R. S., n.d. Robin Sharma. [Online]
Available at: https://www.robinsharma.com/article/burn-your-boats
Hoff, N., 2017. Success. [Online]
Available at: https://www.success.com/to-be-successful-burn-your-boats/

6. Oliver Napoleon Hill
(born 26 October 1883 – 8 November 1970) was an American self-help author. He is known best for his book Think and Grow Rich (1937) which is among the ten bestselling self-help books of all time. Hill's works insisted that fervid expectations are essential to improving one's life. Most of his books were promoted as expounding principles to achieve "success"
Wikipedia, 2020. Wikipedia. [Online]
Available at: https://en.wikipedia.org/wiki/Napoleon_Hill

7. Think and Grow Rich'
Hill, N., 1937. Think and Grow rich. 1st ed. s.l.: The Ralston University Press.

8. "The Sunk Cost Bias"
Sunk costs do, in fact, influence people's decisions, with people believing that investments (i.e., sunk costs) justify further expenditures. People demonstrate "a greater tendency to continue an endeavour once an investment in money, effort, or the time has been made. This is the sunk cost fallacy, and such behaviour may be described as "throwing good money after bad while refusing to succumb to what may be described as "cutting one's losses".
Wikipedia, 2020. Wikipedia. [Online]
Available at: https://en.wikipedia.org/wiki/Sunk_cost#Fallacy_effect

9. J. Nevid

Today, P., n.d. Psychology Today. [Online]
Available at: https://www.psychologytoday.com/za/experts/jeffrey-s-nevid-phd-abpp

10. "Incentives theory" & 11. "Cognitive dissonance theory"

Nevid, J. s., 2007. motivation and emotion. In: 2nd, ed. psychology concepts and application. s.l. Houghton Mifflin Company, pp. 300 -301.

12. Nike

Nike, Inc. is an American multinational corporation that is engaged in the design, development, manufacturing, and worldwide marketing and sales of footwear, apparel, equipment, accessories, and services. The company is headquartered near Beaverton, Oregon, in the Portland metropolitan area. It is the world's largest supplier of athletic shoes and apparel and a major manufacturer of sports equipment.
Wikipedia, 2020. Wikipedia. [Online]
Available at: https://en.wikipedia.org/wiki/Nike,_Inc.

Chapter 5: The Harsh Reality

1. Final Destination

Final Destination. 2000; 2003; 2006; 2009; 2011. [Film] Directed by James Wong, David R. Ellis, Steven Quale. United States of America: New Line Cinema & Zide/ Perry Productions.

2. Coronavirus disease 2019 (COVID-19)

Is an infectious disease caused by severe acute respiratory syndrome coronavirus 2 (SARS-CoV-2). It was first identified in December 2019 in Wuhan, Hubei, China, and has resulted in an ongoing pandemic. The first confirmed case has been traced back to November 2019 in
Hubei. As of July 2020, more than 17 million cases have been reported across 188 countries and territories, resulting in more than 667,000 deaths. More than 9.96 million people have recovered.
Wikipedia, 2020. Wikipedia. [Online]
Available at: https://en.wikipedia.org/wiki/Coronavirus_disease_2019

3.World Health Organisation.

The World Health Organization (WHO) is a specialized agency of the United Nations responsible for international public health. The WHO Constitution, which establishes the agency's governing structure and principles, states its main objective as "the attainment by all peoples of the highest possible level of health." It is headquartered in Geneva, Switzerland, with six semi-autonomous regional offices and 150 field offices worldwide.
https://www.who.int/
Wikipedia, 2020. Wikipedia. [Online]
Available at: https://en.wikipedia.org/wiki/World_Health_Organization

4. Reasons to stay alive, Matt Haig
Haig, M., 2015. Reasons To Stay Alive. 1st ed. s.l.: Canongate Books.

5. Aesop, 1994.
The Cock and The Jewel. In: Aesop's Fables. s.l.: Wordsworth Classics, p. 117.

6. Ikigai
Ikigai is a Japanese concept that means "a reason for being". The word refers to having a direction or purpose in life. That which makes one's life worthwhile, and towards which an individual takes spontaneous and willing actions giving them satisfaction and a sense of meaning to life.

García, H. & Miralles, F., 2017. Ikigai: The Japanese secret to a long and happy life. 1st ed. s.l.: Hutchinson.

Wikipedia, 2020. Wikipedia. [Online]
Available at: https://en.wikipedia.org/wiki/Ikigai

7. The Ohkasi Study
Sone T, Nakaya N, Ohmori K, et al. Sense of life worth living (Ikigai) and mortality in Japan: Ohsaki Study. Psychosom Med. 2008;70(6):709-715. doi:10.1097/PSY.0b013e31817e7e64

8. James Clear
Clear, J., 2018. Atomic Habits. 1st ed. s.l.: Random Penguin House.

9. Schopenhauer
Arthur Schopenhauer (1788 –1860) was a German philosopher. He is best known for his 1818 work The World as Will and Representation (expanded in 1844), wherein he characterizes the phenomenal world as the product of a blind and insatiable metaphysical will. He was among the first thinkers in Western philosophy to share and affirm significant tenets of Indian philosophy, such as asceticism, denial of the self, and the notion of the world-as-appearance. His work has been described as an exemplary manifestation of philosophical pessimism.

10. America's Got Talent
(often abbreviated as AGT) is a televised American talent show competition and is part of the global Got Talent franchise created by Simon Cowell.
Wikipedia, 2020. Wikipedia. [Online]
Available at: https://en.wikipedia.org/wiki/America%27s_Got_Talent

11. The X Factor
Is a television music competition franchise created by British producer Simon Cowell and his company SYCOtv. It originated in the United Kingdom, where it was devised as a replacement for Pop Idol (2001–2003), and has been adapted in various countries. The "X Factor" of the title refers to the undefinable "something" that makes for star quality.
Wikipedia, 2020. Wikipedia. [Online]
Available at: https://en.wikipedia.org/wiki/The_X_Factor

12. Michael Jackson

Michael Joseph Jackson (August 29, 1958 – June 25, 2009) was an American singer, songwriter, and dancer. Dubbed the "King of Pop", he is regarded as one of the most significant cultural figures of the 20th century and one of the greatest entertainers in the history of music. Through stage and video performances, he popularized complicated dance techniques such as the moonwalk, to which he gave the name.

Wikipedia, 2020. Wikipedia. [Online]

Available at: https://en.wikipedia.org/wiki/Michael_jackson

13. Michelle Obama

Michelle LaVaughn Robinson Obama (born January 17, 1964) is an American attorney and author who was the first lady of the United States from 2009 to 2017. She is married to the 44th president of the United States, Barack Obama. She was the first African-American.

Motivation2Study, 2018. YouTube. [Online]

Available at: https://www.youtube.com/watch?v=Rq6CL0nYQnk

14. Facebook Overload

Pantic, Igor. (2014). Online Social Networking and Mental Health. Cyberpsychology, Behaviour, and Social Networking. 17. 10.1089/cyber.2014.0070.

CBS News. [Online]

Available at: https://www.cbsnews.com/pictures/depression-12-sneaky-causes/8/

15. Bitcoin

Bitcoin is a cryptocurrency invented in 2008 by an unknown person or group of people using the name Satoshi Nakamoto and started in 2009 when its implementation was released as open-source software. It is a decentralized digital currency without a central bank or single administrator that can be sent from user to user on the peer-to-peer bitcoin network without the need for intermediaries

Wikipedia, 2020. Wikipedia. [Online]

Available at: https://en.wikipedia.org/wiki/Bitcoin

16. Pablo

Pablo Ruiz Picasso (1881 –1973) was a Spanish painter, sculptor, printmaker, ceramicist and theatre designer who spent most of his adult life in France. Regarded as one of the most influential artists of the 20th century,

Wikipedia, 2020. Wikipedia. [Online]

Available at: https://en.wikipedia.org/wiki/Bitcoin

17. Leonardo

Leonardo da Vinci (April 1452–1519) was an Italian polymath of the High Renaissance who is widely considered one of the greatest painters of all time (despite fewer than 25 of his paintings have survived). The Mona Lisa is the most

famous of Leonardo's works and the most famous portrait ever made.
Wikipedia, 2020. Wikipedia. [Online]
Available at: https://en.wikipedia.org/wiki/Leonardo_da_Vinci

18. Michelangelo
Michelangelo di Lodovico Buonarroti Simoni (1475 −1564), was an Italian sculptor, painter, architect and poet of the High Renaissance born in the Republic of Florence, who exerted an unparalleled influence on the development of Western art.
Wikipedia, 2020. Wikipedia. [Online]
Available at: https://en.wikipedia.org/wiki/Michelangelo

Chapter 6: What to Trust

1. 'The Great Wall of China
The Great Wall of China is the collective name of a series of fortification systems generally built across the historical northern borders of China. They were built to protect and consolidate territories of Chinese states and empires against various nomadic groups of the steppe and their polities.
Geil, B. W. E., 1909. The Great Wall. 1st ed. s.l.: John Murray.
Anon., n.d. China Discovery. [Online]
Available at: https://www.chinadiscovery.com/great-wall/facts/how-long-is-the-great-wall-of-china.html

2. Ecclesiastes4: (Anon., n.d.)
Anon., n.d. Ecclesiastes 9:11. In: The Holy Bible. s.l.:s.n.

Chapter 7: Embracing to Become

1. Stephen R. Covey
Covey, S. R., 2017. The 7 Habits of Highly Effective People. 1st ed. s.l.: FranklinCovey Co.

2. John Broadus Watson (1878 – 1958)
Was an American psychologist who popularized the scientific theory of behaviourism. Watson advanced this change in the psychological discipline through his 1913 address at Columbia University, titled Psychology as the Behaviourist Views It. Through his behaviourist approach, Watson researched animal behaviour, child-rearing, and advertising, as well as conducting the controversial "Little Albert" experiment and the Kerplunk experiment.
Hunt, M., 1993. The story of psychology. 1st ed. s.l.: Anchor Books.
Wikipedia, 2020. Wikipedia. [Online]
Available at: https://en.wikipedia.org/wiki/John_B._Watson

3. Little Albert Experiment
Watson, John & Rayner, Rosalie. (2000). Conditioned emotional reactions. American Psychologist. 55. 313-317. 10.1037/0003-066X.55.3.313.

4. Rosalie Rayner
Rosalie Alberta Rayner (1898 – 1935) was a research psychologist, and the assistant and later wife of psychology professor John B. Watson, with whom she carried out the famous Little Albert experiment.
Wikipedia, 2020. Wikipedia. [Online]
Available at: https://en.wikipedia.org/wiki/Rosalie_Rayner

5. Classical Conditioning
Nevid, J. S., 2007. Learning. In: 2nd, ed. Psychology concept and applications. s.l.: Houghton Mifflin, pp. 182-207

6. Trial and Error.
Trial and Error is a fundamental method of problem-solving. It is characterized by repeated, varied attempts which are continued until success, or until the practicer stops trying.
Wikipedia, 2020. Wikipedia. [Online]
Available at: https://en.wikipedia.org/wiki/Trial_and_error

7. Thomas Alva Edison
Was an American inventor and businessman who has been described as America's greatest inventor.

8. "practically beyond attainment."
Dyer, F. L. & Martin, T. C., 2010. Edison, His Life and Inventions. 2nd ed. s.l.: The Floating Press.

9. Utopia
A utopia is an imagined community or society that possesses highly desirable or nearly perfect qualities for its citizens. The term was coined by Sir Thomas More for his 1516 book Utopia, describing a fictional island society in the south Atlantic Ocean off the coast of South America. The opposite of a utopia is a dystopia, which dominates the fictional literature.
Wikipedia, 2020. Wikipedia. [Online]
Available at: https://en.wikipedia.org/wiki/Utopia

10. Magic of thinking big
Schwartz, D. J., 2016. Cure yourself from excusitis, the failure disease. In: The Magic of Thinking Big. s.l.: Vermilion London, p. 49.

11. Joanne Rowling (born 31 July 1965)
Better known by her pen name J. K. Rowling, is a British author, screenwriter, producer, and philanthropist. She is best known for writing the Harry Potter fantasy series, which has won multiple awards. It has also sold more than 500 million copies, becoming the best-selling book series in history. The books are the basis of a popular film series, over which Rowling had overall approval on the scripts and was a producer on the final films.
https://www.jkrowling.com/about/
https://www.forbes.com/profile/jk-rowling/#195bf0c43aeb

Wikipedia, 2020. Wikipedia. [Online]
Available at: https://en.wikipedia.org/wiki/J._K._Rowling

12. Glenn Cunningham

Rogers, T., 1988. Obituaries. [Online]
Available at: https://www.nytimes.com/1988/03/11/obituaries/glenn-cunningham-78-premier-miler-of-1930-s.html
Britannica, T. E. o. E., 2020. Encylopedia Britannica. [Online]
Available at: https://www.britannica.com/biography/Glenn-Cunningham

13. Theodore Roosevelt

Theodore Roosevelt Jr. (1858 – 1919), often referred to as Teddy Roosevelt or his initials T. R., was an American statesman, politician, conservationist, naturalist, and writer. He served as the 26th president of the United States from 1901 to 1909. He served as the 25th vice president from March to September 1901 and as the 33rd governor of New York from 1899 to 1900.

Wikipedia, 2020. Wikipedia. [Online]
Available at: https://en.wikipedia.org/wiki/Theodore_Roosevelt

14. Man in the arena

Citizenship in a Republic is the title of a speech given by Theodore Roosevelt, former President of the United States, at the Sorbonne in Paris, France, on 23 April 1910.

One notable passage on page seven of the 35-page speech is referred to as "The Man in the Arena"

Wikipedia, 2020. Wikipedia. [Online]
Available at: https://en.wikipedia.org/wiki/Citizenship_in_a_Republic

15. Toastmasters International Club.

Toastmasters International (TI) is a US-headquartered non-profit educational organization that operates clubs worldwide for the purpose of promoting communication, public speaking and leadership.

Toastmasters, 2020. Toastmasters International. [Online]
Available at: https://www.toastmasters.org/

16. Trent Simmons Shelton (born 21 September 1984)

Is a former American football wide receiver. He is currently the founder and President of a Christian-based non-profit organization, RehabTime. During March 2009 Shelton started making two-minute videos to track his progress of bettering his life and would always end the videos with, "It's RehabTime." He was raised in Fort Worth, Texas, and wanted to become a professional football player when he grew up.

https://www.trentshelton.com/home
Wikipedia, 2020. Wikipedia. [Online]
Available at: https://en.wikipedia.org/wiki/Trent_Shelton

17. Joseph
In the biblical narrative, Joseph was sold into slavery by his jealous brothers and rose to become vizier, the second most powerful man in Egypt next to Pharaoh.
Wikipedia, 2020. Wikipedia. [Online]
Available at: https://en.wikipedia.org/wiki/Joseph_(Genesis)

18. Genesis (Anon., n.d.)
Anon., n.d. Genesis 37 -50. In: The Holy Bible. s.l.:s.n.

Chapter 8: Becoming to Lead

1. William Kamkwamba
Refer to Chapter 1

2. Parable of the Talents
Anon., n.d. Matthew 25:14–30. In: The Holy Bible. s.l.:s.n.

3. The Matthew effect of accumulated advantage, Matthew principle, or Matthew effect for short
Is sometimes summarized by the adage "the rich get richer and, the poor get poorer." The concept is applicable to matters of fame or status, but may also be applied literally to the cumulative advantage of economic capital. Matthew's effects were primarily focused on inequality in the way scientists were recognized for their work.
Anon., n.d. Matthew 25:14–30. In: The Holy Bible. s.l.:s.n.

4. Nikolayevich Tolstoy (1828 –1910)
Was a Russian writer who is regarded as one of the greatest authors of all time. He received multiple nominations for the Nobel Peace Prize in Literature every year from 1902 to 1906 and nominations for the Nobel Peace Prize in 1901, 1902 and 1910. The fact that he never won is a major Nobel Prize controversy.
Wikipedia, 2020. Wikipedia. [Online]
Available at: https://en.wikipedia.org/wiki/Leo_Tolstoy

5. Mohandas Karamchand Gandhi (1869 –1948)
Was an Indian lawyer, anti-colonial nationalist, and political ethicist. He employed nonviolent resistance to lead the successful a campaign for India's independence from British Rule, and in turn, inspired movements for civil rights and freedom across the world.
Wikipedia, 2020. Wikipedia. [Online]
Available at: https://en.wikipedia.org/wiki/Mahatma_Gandhi

6. Martin Luther King Jr. (1929 –1968)
Was an African American minister and activist who became the most visible spokesperson and leader in the civil rights movement from 1955 until his assassination in 1968. King is best known for advancing civil rights through nonviolence and civil disobedience, inspired by his Christian beliefs and the nonviolent activism of Mahatma Gandhi.

King led the 1955 Montgomery bus boycott and later became the first president of the Southern Christian Leadership Conference (SCLC). He helped organize the 1963 March on Washington, where he delivered his famous "I Have a Dream" speech on the Lincoln Memorial steps.

Wikipedia, 2020. Wikipedia. [Online]

Available at: https://en.wikipedia.org/wiki/Martin_Luther_King_Jr.

7. Ralph Waldo Emerson (1803 –1882)

Was an American essayist, lecturer, philosopher, and poet who led the transcendentalist movement of the mid-19th century. He was seen as a champion of individualism and a prescient critic of society's countervailing pressures, and he disseminated his thoughts through dozens of published essays and more than 1,500 public lectures across the United States.

Wikipedia, 2020. Wikipedia. [Online]

Available at: https://en.wikipedia.org/wiki/Ralph_Waldo_Emerson

8. Jesus

Also referred to as Jesus of Nazareth or Jesus Christ, was a first-century Jewish preacher and religious leader. He is the central figure of Christianity. Most Christians believe he is the incarnation of God the Son and the awaited Messiah (the Christ) prophesied in the Old Testament.

Anon., n.d. The Holy Bible. s.l.:s.n.

Wikipedia, 2020. Wikipedia. [Online]

Available at: https://en.wikipedia.org/wiki/Jesus

9. The Buddha (also known as Siddhattha Gotama or Siddhārtha Gautama)

Was a philosopher, mendicant, meditator, spiritual teacher, and religious leader who lived in Ancient India. He is revered as the founder of the world religion of Buddhism. He taught for around 45 years and built a large following, both monastic and lay. His teaching is based on his insight into duḥkha (typically translated as "suffering") and the end of dukkha – the state called Nibbāna or Nirvana.

Siridhamma, R., n.d. The Life of Buddha. 1st ed. s.l.: Buddhist Missionary Society.

Wikipedia, 2020. Wikipedia. [Online]

Available at: https://en.wikipedia.org/wiki/Gautama_Buddha

10. Muhammad

Was an Arab religious, social, and political leader and the founder of Islam. According to Islamic doctrine, he was a prophet, sent to preach and confirm the monotheistic teachings of Adam, Abraham, Moses, Jesus, and other prophets. He is viewed as the final prophet of God in all the main branches of Islam, though some modern denominations diverge from this belief. Muhammad united Arabia into a single Muslim polity, with the Quran, as well as his teachings and practices, forming the basis of Islamic religious belief.

Wikipedia, 2020. Wikipedia. [Online]

Available at: https://en.wikipedia.org/wiki/Muhammad

11. The Miller, His Son & Their Ass
Aesop, 1994. The Miller, His Son & Their Ass. In: Aesop's Fables. s.l.: Wordsworth Classics, p. 130.

Chapter 9: Becoming Happy
1. Positive Psychology
Positive psychology is the scientific study of the "good life", or the positive aspects of the human experience that make life worth living. The discipline of positive psychology focuses on both individual and societal well-being.
Wikipedia, 2020. Wikipedia. [Online]
Available at: https://en.wikipedia.org/wiki/Positive_psychology

2. King Midas
Britannica, T. E. o. E., 2020. Encyclopaedia Britannica. [Online]
Available at: https://www.britannica.com/topic/Midas-Greek-mythology#info-article-history

3. Studies On happiness
Heather Craig, B., 2020. Positive Psychology. [Online]
Available at: https://positivepsychology.com/psychology-of-happiness/
Kahneman, Daniel & Deaton, Angus. (2010). High Income Improves Evaluation of Life But Not Emotional Well-Being. Proceedings of the National Academy of Sciences of the United States of America. 107. 16489-93. 10.1073/pnas.1011492107.

4. Norrish, Jacolyn & Vella-Brodrick, Dianne. (2007).
Is the Study of Happiness a Worthy Scientific Pursuit?. Social Indicators Research. 87. 393-407. 10.1007/s11205-007-9147-x.

5. 'Top Five Regrets of the Dying'
Ware, B., 2019. The Top 5 Regrets of the Dying. 2nd ed. s.l.: Hay House, Inc.

6. Aristotle
Aristotle was a Greek philosopher and polymath during the Classical period in Ancient Greece. His writings cover many subjects including physics, biology, zoology, metaphysics, logic, ethics, aesthetics, poetry, theatre, music, rhetoric, psychology, linguistics, economics, politics, and government.

7. S. Covey
See Chapter 2

8. Will Smith - "her happiness is not my responsibility"
Willard Carroll Smith Jr. (born September 25, 1968) is an American actor, producer and rapper. In April 2007, Newsweek called him "the most powerful actor in Hollywood". Smith has been nominated for five Golden Globe Awards and two Academy Awards and has won four Grammy Awards.
Carra, T., 2018. Haute Living. [Online]
Available at: https://hauteliving.com/2018/02/will-smith-jada-pinkett-smith/651889/
Brand, T. J., 2018. YouTube. [Online]
Available at: https://www.youtube.com/watch?v=nUwzrqcPujg

9. Nirvana
Is a transcendent state in which there is neither suffering, desire, nor sense of self. It represents the final goal of Buddhism.

10.   The Hedonic Treadmill
The hedonic treadmill, also known as hedonic adaptation, is the observed tendency of humans to quickly return to a relatively stable level of happiness despite major positive or negative events or life changes. According to this theory, as a person makes more money, expectations and desires rise in tandem, which results in no permanent gain in happiness.

Wikipedia, 2020. Wikipedia. [Online]

Available at: https://en.wikipedia.org/wiki/Hedonic_treadmill

11. Research carried out by Brickman and Campbell in 1971
Brickman, Philip & Coates, Dan & Janoff-Bulman, Ronnie. (1978). Lottery Winners and Accident Victims: Is Happiness Relative? Journal of personality and social psychology. 36. 917-27. 10.1037/0022-3514.36.8.917.

12. Diener, Ed & Lucas, R & Scollon, Christie. (2006). Beyond the hedonic treadmill. American Psychologist. 61. 305-314.

13. Study of identical twins.
Tellegen, Auke & Lykken, David & Bouchard Jr, Thomas & Wilcox, Kimerly & Segal, Nancy & Rich, Stephen. (1988). Personality Similarity in Twins Reared Apart and Together. Journal of Personality and Social Psychology. 54. 1031-1039. 10.1037/0022-3514.54.6.1031.

14. A 2005 study carried out by Fujita and Diener
Fujita, Frank & Diener, Ed. (2005). Life Satisfaction Set Point: Stability and Change. Journal of personality and social psychology. 88. 158-64. 10.1037/0022-3514.88.1.158.

15. Lucas, R. E., Clark, A. E., Georgellis, Y., & Diener, E. (2003).
Reexamining adaptation and the set point model of happiness: Reactions to changes in marital status. Journal of Personality and Social Psychology, 84(3), 527–539. https://doi.org/10.1037/0022-3514.84.3.527

Chapter 10: The Art of Becoming

1. Captain America
See Chapter 7

2. Marvel's The Avengers or simply The Avengers
Is a 2012 American superhero film based on the Marvel Comics superhero team of the same name.

The Avengers. 2012. [Film] Directed by Joss Whedon. USA: Marvel Studios.

3. Hein Wagner
See Chapter 1

4. Lena Salmi
See Chapter 1